THE COURAGE
TO
CARE

Stories of Healing, Hope, and the Power of Social Work

Told by Over 50 SWEET Institute Social Workers

Edited by

Karen Dubin, Ph.D., LCSW,

and Mardoche Sidor, MD

SWEET Institute Publishing

Transformational Books for a Transformational World.

Published by:

SWEET Institute Publishing

New York, NY

WWW.SWEETInstitutePublishing.com

First Edition

Printed in the United States of America

ISBN (Paperback): 978-1-968105-01-3

Cover Design: SWEET Institute Publishing

Interior Design and Layout: SWEET Institute Publishing

For bulk orders, permissions, or media inquiries, please contact:

info@sweetinstitutepublishing.com

Unless otherwise noted, all stories and case examples in this book are either fictionalized or used with permission, and identifying details have been changed to protect the privacy of individuals.

SWEET Institute Publishing

Transformational Books for a Transformational World

Dedication

To all who have had the courage to care—
for themselves, for others, and for the world.

And to every social worker, clinician, healer, and advocate
who dares to stand beside those who suffer
and believes in their power to heal.

Table of Contents

Foreword by Jules Ranz, MD

Professor of Psychiatry, Columbia University Vagelos College of Physicians and Surgeons

Former Director, Columbia Public Psychiatry Fellowship

Over the course of my career, I've had the honor of working with dedicated professionals across a wide spectrum of mental health disciplines—psychiatrists, social workers, psychologists, nurse practitioners, peer specialists, and more. In these collaborations, I've found a consistent truth: at the heart of mental health care, it is the social workers who often carry the connective tissue of our systems. They are the thread between diagnosis and housing, between theory and lived experience, between suffering and the possibility of healing.

That's why The Courage to Care is such a timely and necessary book.

This collection of stories—authentic, vulnerable, deeply human—reveals the full complexity of what it means to serve others while remaining grounded in one's own values, history, and growth. It invites us into the real lives and inner worlds of 50 social workers from the SWEET Institute—a group I've been privileged to support and witness firsthand.

In these pages, you will not find a sanitized or overly theoretical presentation of social work. Instead, you will encounter what I believe is the most important ingredient in any helping profession: integrity of purpose. You'll read about early influences, moments of doubt, ethical crossroads, healing breakthroughs, and bold visions for the future of our field.

What makes this book truly remarkable is not just its range of stories—it's the depth of reflection and the commitment to transformation that runs through them. These clinicians don't merely recount experiences. They integrate them—with humility, intellectual rigor, and a relentless pursuit of excellence.

This is the very spirit that defined the Columbia Public Psychiatry Fellowship for decades: the integration of personal insight, interdisciplinary collaboration, and a commitment to systems-level impact.

The SWEET Institute has taken this ethos and amplified it. With an emphasis on adult learning, experiential reflection, and a model that bridges theory and practice, the Institute has created a community where clinicians are not only trained—they are awakened. And that awakening radiates outward: to their colleagues, their organizations, and most importantly, to the individuals and families they serve.

I believe this book will resonate not just with social workers, but with anyone who cares about the soul of mental health care. At a time when our systems are often strained, bureaucratized, and dehumanizing, The Courage to Care is a reminder of what is possible when professionals are empowered, seen, and supported in bringing their full selves to the work.

This book is more than a tribute. It is a blueprint—a living example of what can happen when we invest in the human beings who hold the line, ask the hard questions, and walk alongside those society too often overlooks.

To the SWEET Institute clinicians who opened their hearts to write these stories, and to the editors who shaped them with such care: Thank you. You've given us a book that teaches, heals, and dares us to reimagine what mental health care can be.

Jules Ranz, MD
Professor of Psychiatry
Columbia University Vagelos College of Physicians and Surgeons

Preface by Dr. Claire Green-Forde, LCSW

Founder & CEO | Dr. Claire SPEAKS! LLC

When I think about the work we do as social workers, I'm reminded that it's not just a profession, it's a calling. One that chooses us, sometimes in ways we never expect, but always in ways that shape who we are. We choose to show up, day after day, to be present in the lives of those who need us the most. But behind every act of care, there is a person who, just like those we serve, needs care too.

As social workers, we are often the ones holding space for others' pain, joy, and transformation; we must never forget that our own transformation and healing is just as essential. *We cannot be the vessels of healing for others if we are not nourishing our own well-being*, tending to our own humanity, and advocating for ourselves with the same courage we offer to those we serve.

I had the privilege of reading some of the interviews featured in this book and I was moved by their rawness, power, and the deeply transformative nature of each story. These voices reminded me of why I answered the call, and they serve as a reminder of our collective "why" as social workers. These are stories of humanity, stories of immigrants, of resilience in systems built for failure, of efforts to center humanity in a world that often strips us of it. I saw myself in every narrative, in the trauma, the healing, the fight for justice, and the need for rest.

Social work is not a 9-to-5 job. It's a way of being. To truly be a social worker, it's not simply about the degree we earn, it's about living out the values of our profession, both publicly and privately. It's about being bold in our advocacy, brave in confronting the biases we carry, and embracing the responsibility to center humanity in everything we do. It's about honoring the dignity and worth of every individual, as our code of ethics urges us. But let's be clear, this call to advocacy has been silenced over the years, and we can no longer afford to let it be. Not in a world that is in pain, and not in a profession that sometimes causes us pain.

While I may not know the incredible humans featured in this book personally, I saw aspects of myself in each of their stories. I saw the same struggles, the same triumphs, the same need to return to our roots of advocacy, compassion, innovation, leadership, and love. This is not one story: it's all our stories. It's the complexity of human experience, with all its nuances, pain, hope, and healing. To truly do this work, to change systems and transform lives, we must begin by transforming ourselves. We must take care of our own well-being, we must advocate for our own needs, and we must commit to building community beyond our own circles of comfort. If we are to shift the world, we must learn to step outside of our own demographics, our own lived experiences, and build connections that allow us to experience the world through different perspectives.

As you read these stories, I encourage you to reflect on your own journey and ask yourself: How am I taking care of myself? How am I living out the values of social work? How am I living in a way that honors the humanity of those I serve, and my own?

This is a call to return to our roots of care, advocacy, and love; to do that, we must start with ourselves, and we must do it consistently. The Courage to Care begins with us and only by nurturing our own humanity can we make a difference in the lives of others.

With appreciation and in solidarity,

Dr. Claire Green-Forde, LCSW
Founder & CEO I Dr. Claire SPEAKS! LLC

Reflections by Karen Dubin, PhD, LCSW

"Social work is not just a profession — it is a way of being."

The Courage to Care began as a simple idea: to gather and honor the stories of social workers—stories too often left untold. But as I embarked on this journey, what unfolded was far more than a collection of interviews. It became a path of rediscovery—a way back to myself.

Over the course of a year, I had the profound privilege of sitting with more than fifty clinicians from the SWEET community, listening not only to their professional narratives but to the lives behind the labels. With each conversation, I didn't just hear their stories—I saw my own reflection. In the social worker who stumbled into the field, I recognized the younger version of myself who once believed this work had found her by accident. In the advocate fighting tirelessly within broken systems, I saw my own fire. And in the one who had come to see their identity as inseparable from the calling of social work, I found my truth.

These interviews were more than documentation—they were mirrors. They illuminated something I had long forgotten: that I have always been on this path. Not by chance, but by purpose.

The SWEET Institute believes that to truly support others, we must also support ourselves. We must be seen. We must be heard. And we must gather—not just as professionals, but as people whose stories shape how we serve.

What emerged from these interviews was not just a series of individual narratives, but a living, breathing mosaic of vulnerability, strength, struggle, and hope. These clinicians did not present themselves as heroes, but as humans—honest, complex, and deeply committed.

Each section of this book reflects a different part of the journey—why we begin, what shapes us, how we continue, and where we dream of going. And in that reflection, I found myself. Perhaps, as you turn these pages, you will too.

This is not just a book about social work. It is a book about life—about choosing to show up, day after day, with open eyes and an open heart, in service of healing, justice, and deep connection. It is about remembering who we are, why we do this work, and the shared humanity that binds us all.

So welcome—welcome to The Courage to Care. May it remind you that your story matters too.

Karen Dubin, PhD, LCSW
COO & Co-Founder ~ SWEET Institute

Reflections by Mardoche Sidor, MD

In a time when the world urgently needs healing, understanding, and connection, this book offers a powerful testament to the enduring strength and wisdom of the social work profession. It is not just a compilation of stories—it is a living archive of courage, reflection, transformation, and truth.

What you are about to read is extraordinary. Over 50 clinicians, each walking their own unique path, opened their hearts and minds to share not only what they do, but who they are. They speak to the origin of their purpose, the challenges they've faced, the healing they've facilitated, and the deep personal meaning behind their professional identities. Their voices—raw, nuanced, and profoundly human—resonate with the shared essence of the SWEET Institute's mission: to support, empower, and elevate mental health professionals through connection, community, and consciousness.

These stories go beyond the clinical. They are rooted in humanity. They offer wisdom to the next generation and affirmation to the current one. They remind us that social work is not just a profession—it is a calling. And like all true callings, it evolves, deepens, and expands through community.

This book stands as a landmark—not only for the SWEET Institute, but for the field of social work and mental health as a whole. It invites us to reflect, to grow, and most importantly, to remember why we chose this path in the first place.

Welcome to a journey of shared purpose, deep insight, and radical hope.

Mardoche Sidor, MD
Quadruple Board-Certified Psychiatrist
Columbia University & SWEET Institute
Medical Director, Urban Pathways

Introduction

Social work is often described as both a science and an art. It is a discipline rooted in theory, driven by evidence, and practiced through the lens of human experience. But at its core, social work is also a calling—one that demands presence, courage, compassion, and an unwavering belief in the possibility of change.

This book began with a question: What if we paused long enough to ask the healers how they are shaped? Not just by their training or their work, but by their own lived experiences. What if we listened to the social workers—not just as professionals—but as people who bring their whole selves to the work?

Over the span of two years, we engaged more than 50 clinicians in one-on-one conversations. These were not surveys or interviews in the traditional sense. They were dialogues. Invitations. Explorations. The clinicians who participated did so with radical honesty, vulnerability, and a desire to contribute something meaningful to the field and to one another.

Their stories reflect a diversity of identities, backgrounds, and clinical settings—from schools to hospitals, courtrooms to community centers. But across this range, one theme emerged with clarity: social work is deeply human work. And the people who do it are continually evolving.

You will not find prescriptive techniques in these pages. Instead, you will find reflection, insight, and lived wisdom. You will hear from clinicians who navigated childhood trauma and turned it into purpose. From those who pivoted careers midlife to follow a deeper call. From seasoned therapists still learning to trust their voice. From advocates, educators, and leaders envisioning the future of our profession.

This book is structured to honor the phases of the social work journey: the beginnings, the formative experiences, the modalities of practice, the communities of support, the insights they pass on, and the meaning they make of it all. Each section weaves together individual voices into collective chapters— portraits of our field as it is and as it could be.

We hope this book becomes more than a reading experience. May it become a mirror. A conversation. A space for you to reflect on your own path, your own wisdom, and your place within this remarkable community.

Why This Book

The field of social work is facing a pivotal moment. As systems become more complex, inequities deepen, and burnout grows, many clinicians are asking themselves: Why did I choose this path? How do I stay grounded in purpose? And where do we go from here?

This book was created in response to those questions. Not to provide easy answers, but to create a space for reflection, solidarity, and renewal. In our daily practice, we hold the stories of others. We bear witness to trauma, to resilience, to transformation. But rarely do we turn that same lens inward—to reflect on how our own stories shape the care we provide.

We wanted to change that.

Through more than fifty in-depth conversations with SWEET Institute members—social workers, counselors, advocates, educators, and leaders—we gathered the untold stories of those who have committed their lives to service. What we found was both humbling and inspiring: people who are navigating immense challenges with courage and creativity, people who are transforming pain into purpose, and people who are shaping the future of mental health and social services with compassion, vision, and resolve.

This book is a celebration of them—and of you.

Whether you're just beginning your career or are decades into practice, whether you work in direct service, policy, education, or leadership, this book is meant to reflect your experience and invite your voice. It honors the fullness of our journeys and reminds us that we are never alone in this work.

In these pages, you will find shared humanity. You will find questions worth asking. And you will find—above all—a community committed to healing, learning, and creating lasting change.

This book exists because stories matter. Yours included.

How This Book Came About

This book began as a question and an intention: What would happen if we paused long enough to really listen to each other—not as experts or professionals, but as human beings walking a shared path?

That question emerged from within the SWEET Institute—a community dedicated not just to teaching evidence-based mental health care, but to embodying a new paradigm of learning, transformation, and service. Over the years, the SWEET community has grown to include thousands of clinicians across disciplines, geographies, and life experiences. What unites them is a commitment to continuous learning, to compassionate care, and to becoming who they are meant to be.

In 2024, we embarked on a process of deep listening. More than 50 SWEET clinicians were invited to participate in in-depth, one-on-one interviews—each a sacred space for reflection, vulnerability, and storytelling. These were not surveys. These were not scripted conversations. These were dialogues rooted in presence, trust, and a shared desire to illuminate the heart of this work.

Each interview yielded a story—sometimes simple, sometimes profound, always human. These stories were then curated, categorized, and gently woven into themes that reflected both the personal and the collective: Why they entered the field. What shaped their clinical identity. The moments that nearly broke them—and the ones that built them. Their beliefs, their hopes, and their visions for the future.

We did not write this book about them. We wrote it with them.

Every chapter is infused with their voice. Every insight is grounded in lived experience. And every section honors the integrity and generosity of each clinician who trusted us with their story.

This is more than a compilation. It is a mosaic. A tapestry of lived wisdom. A mirror for those who seek to serve—and to remember why.

How to Read This Book

This book is not a manual, and it's not meant to be read in one sitting—though you might be tempted.

It is a living archive. A mirror. A circle of voices meant to accompany you in your own journey as a clinician, a healer, a human being.

You can read this book cover to cover, following the carefully structured flow from origin stories to visions of the future. Doing so reveals the arc of transformation that runs through our field—from the first spark of inspiration to the challenges and revelations of practice, the evolution of therapeutic craft, the power of community, and the soul of this work.

Or you can read it thematically—dip into the chapters that speak to your present moment. Perhaps you're feeling weary, and the section on burnout and boundaries will feel like balm. Or maybe you're exploring new clinical modalities, and the pages on innovation and integration will offer insight and encouragement. Maybe you simply want to feel less alone—and any chapter will serve as a hand extended.

Each chapter can stand alone. But together, they create a chorus.

Here are a few ways to engage with this book:

- As a source of reflection – Use it during supervision, study groups, or personal journaling. Let the clinicians' words prompt your own.
- As a learning companion – Read it alongside clinical training to ground theory in lived experience.
- As a call to action – Let it remind you of what's possible, what's urgent, and what's worth building.
- As a quiet friend – Return to it when the work feels heavy. Let it lift you.

Most importantly: read it as you. There is no one right way to hold these stories—only an invitation to honor them as you would your own.

This book is an offering. May it nourish, challenge, affirm, and ignite something sacred within you.

Acknowledgments

This book would not have been possible without the generosity, vulnerability, and courage of over 50 SWEET Institute members who shared their stories, struggles, and insights with the hope of lighting the path for others.

We extend our deepest gratitude to:

Adaiah Lassalle

Agnes Timberger

Alishka Ostrander

Ann-Elizabeth Straub

AnnMarie Tresca

Carrie Miceli

Cheryl Mchunguzi

Daniel Sheehan

Dara Caputo

Deirdra Powell-Robinson

Denise Erker

Devorah Bodenheim

DonnaSue Johnson

Douglas Greenberg

Emmanuel Charles

Eugenia Rosenberg

Grace Paradiso

Guillermina Ceballos

Imee Hernandez

Ines Mercedes Alcantara

Jay Korman

Jeanne Weiner

Jenna Tine

Jose Vasquez

Joy-Hee Lee

Karen Felton Handley

Karen Sumpter

Kathy Pierson

Lisa Marie Sokolowski

Lorie Meiselman

Lydia Watling

Lynwana Johnson

Margaret Michael-Ralston

Marisha Krupkin

Marsha Reed

Michelle Alexander

Monique Anderson

Olivia Holden

Paul Selino

Ruth Smith

Sarah Russ

Scott Christnelly

Shannon Cullen

Sol Reyes Pelosi

Someeka Washington

Steven Herbst

Stuart Aaronson

Sunita Bechan

Vilma Martinez

Yokasta Lopez-Irving

Your honesty, brilliance, and dedication to this work and this world have left an indelible mark.

To all of you who shared their stories with courage, candor, and depth—thank you. This book would not exist without your willingness to be seen, to reflect openly, and to give of yourselves so generously. You trusted this process and, in doing so, created something that will inspire, affirm, and transform others for years to come.

You brought your full humanity to these pages—your early memories, your moments of clarity, your personal struggles, your most meaningful breakthroughs, and your visions for the future of our field. You reminded us that social work is not just a profession, but a calling. Not just a service, but a sacred encounter.

We honor your willingness to be vulnerable.

We honor your commitment to truth.

We honor your dedication to healing—not only for others, but for yourselves and your communities.

Each of you has helped co-create a work that is more than a book—it is a collective remembrance, a movement, a map.

And to every clinician reading this book: thank you for being part of this story, for carrying the work forward, and for staying close to what matters most.

With deepest respect and unwavering gratitude,

We acknowledge you all.

Section 1: Why They Became a Social Worker

Introduction:

Every journey begins with a question—sometimes whispered in a moment of stillness, sometimes shouted in the aftermath of adversity. For the social workers in this collection, the question was often the same: How can I serve? This section explores the origin stories of these dedicated clinicians—stories of inspiration, clarity, struggle, and change. Each chapter unveils a different doorway through which they entered the world of social work, revealing the deeply personal and often unexpected roots of their professional calling. These are not just career decisions; they are acts of becoming.

Section I

Part I

Chapter 1: Early Inspirations and Life Events

Introduction:

In many cases, the impulse to help others begins early. Whether shaped by family, childhood experiences, or cultural immersion, these clinicians found the seeds of social work planted long before formal education began. In this chapter, we meet individuals whose earliest memories of compassion, inclusion, and resilience became the quiet foundation for a life in service.

The seeds of service planted early in life—through family, community, and profound formative experiences.

For many of the clinicians featured in this chapter, the roots of their calling to social work were planted long before graduate school or field placements. These origins often appeared in the form of quiet but meaningful moments in childhood, deeply influential family dynamics, or formative community experiences. These early touchpoints didn't always declare themselves as a "career path," but they embedded a deep sense of empathy, justice, curiosity, and care that would one day blossom into a professional identity.

AnnMarie

Raised in a diverse family, AnnMarie's home was a place of open hearts and open doors—especially to foster children who became like siblings. This spirit of inclusivity left an indelible mark, planting the seeds of her future calling. Although she would not pursue formal training until the age of 42, the richness of her early life—combined with her love for children and creativity—became the foundation for a career defined by advocacy, connection, and purpose.

Adaiah

A chance encounter with a lonely stranger during her childhood revealed to Adaiah the profound impact of empathy. As a teen, she embraced peer counseling, realizing her innate capacity to listen, connect, and guide. Long before she studied psychology or facilitated parent recovery groups, Adaiah's sense of service was already alive—tender, intuitive, and fiercely present.

Karen S

Raised in a challenging environment, Karen found light in the example of a social worker who helped her family during a difficult time. That early experience didn't just make an impression—it planted a conviction. Her journey into social work became a way of paying it forward, embodying the very care and compassion that once changed her life.

Margaret

With a father who was a child psychologist, Margaret grew up immersed in conversations about human behavior, development, and care. Though initially drawn to psychology, she found herself captivated by the diverse and dynamic nature of social work. For her, this wasn't just a career choice—it was a continuation of a family legacy of understanding and healing.

Shannon

From organizing babysitting camps at age 11 to working with children with disabilities at summer camps, Shannon's love for children and her natural leadership emerged early. While she initially pursued school psychology, it was her early hands-on experiences that revealed where her heart truly lay—in forming meaningful, long-term therapeutic relationships with youth.

Imee

Growing up in Sunset Park, Brooklyn, Imee's life was touched early by the transformative presence of Sister Geraldine and Sister Mary Paul at the Center for Family Life. These women not only introduced her to the values of community-based social work—they believed in her, mentored her, and helped her envision a different future. From their example, she inherited a spirit of service that would come to define her life's work.

Jay

Jay's path was shaped by the compassion of a therapist who supported him during a difficult time in his life. That early experience of being truly seen and helped sowed the seed for his own commitment to clinical work. For Jay, social work became a natural extension of gratitude—an ongoing act of paying forward the healing he once received.

Grace

Working in psychosocial programs in the mid-1980s, Grace encountered clients with severe mental illness—individuals often dismissed by society, but who deeply moved her with their stories and complexity. Her early fascination with psychology was deepened by these encounters and by personal loss. Her brother's passing just before college shaped her drive to pursue education despite her parents' opposition. This early combination of personal pain and professional exposure became the fertile ground for her career.

Jeanne

As a child, Jeanne felt different—being very short gave her a sense of otherness that turned into insight. Over time, she began to see this difference as a strength that allowed her to connect more deeply with others. Her love for people and her capacity to listen were present early on and continued to grow through education and fieldwork. Her journey reflects the way lived experience can shape therapeutic sensitivity and relational intelligence.

Olivia

In high school, Olivia dreamed of becoming a psychotherapist, but she pursued dance instead—an artistic path where she could explore expression and emotion through movement. Yet, even as she performed on stage, the pull toward inner transformation lingered. When an injury interrupted her dance career, it became the portal back to her original dream. Looking back, it was clear: her desire to understand the mind had always been part of her.

Stuart

At Brandeis University, Stuart's involvement in encounter groups, anti-war activism, and theater opened his eyes to the complexities of human interaction and systems. These early experiences taught him about vulnerability, expression, and the power of collective healing. Even before he officially entered the field, Stuart was practicing the foundational elements of social work—empathy, reflection, and deep engagement with human systems.

Chapter 2: Moments of Clarity or Calling

Introduction:

Sometimes, a single moment changes everything. A conversation, a crisis, a shift in perspective—these clinicians describe powerful turning points when their purpose became clear. These are stories of revelation, where an inner voice or external sign pointed the way, and life began to align with calling.

The pivotal realizations—life-altering moments when everything aligned and the path became clear.

Sometimes, we spend years circling around a truth that reveals itself in an instant. For the clinicians in this chapter, that moment of clarity came like a spark—an experience, a conversation, a crisis, or a shift that illuminated their path and aligned their life's work with their inner compass. These are the stories of awakening, when vocation stopped being a vague notion and became a clear, unwavering commitment.

Jay

For Jay, it was the transformative experience of being helped by a compassionate therapist during a personal crisis that first lit the fire. That singular experience awakened something within him—a desire to extend the same kind of support to others. The moment was not just healing; it was catalytic. From then on, every step of his academic and clinical journey was rooted in that deeply personal act of reciprocity.

Steven

Sometimes a casual conversation reveals a deeper truth. For Steven, it came during a late-night call with a friend who was struggling. After listening deeply and offering presence, his friend felt relieved and said, "You'd be a great therapist." That offhand comment hit home. Steven—surrounded by family in mental health—decided to reach out to a psychotherapist who affirmed his instincts. In that moment, a path he hadn't previously considered became clear, and he followed it with conviction.

Someeka

Someeka's moment of clarity came in a hospital room, watching over her ailing aunt. There, she observed the social worker's role—not as an administrator or bystander, but as a true advocate and support system. That interaction became a turning point. Though she had initially been drawn to nursing, the social worker's presence showed her a different kind of healing—one that met people at the intersection of systems, emotion, and empowerment.

Olivia

For Olivia, the turning point was as physical as it was existential: an injury that ended her dance career and forced her to reevaluate what she truly wanted. It led her back to a long-standing desire to explore the human psyche. This unexpected rupture became a portal to rediscovery. The clarity she found through her own therapy deepened her sense of purpose, and she committed herself fully to the path of mental health care.

Sarah

Sarah entered college believing she'd become a teacher, but as she examined what truly lit her up, she realized that traditional education felt too rigid. A college advisor introduced her to the world of social work—a field where she could bring her whole self and help others navigate life's complexities in real time. That introduction sparked a new direction, one that immediately felt more aligned with her personality, purpose, and strengths.

Vilma

Vilma had already lived a full life—as a legal secretary and mother of five—before her calling to social work became clear. That moment came when her supervisor, and later a neighbor, encouraged her to pursue the field. Their confidence in her mirrored something she had long sensed but never named.

Once she stepped into the role of a case manager, everything clicked. Helping young mothers navigate uncertainty ignited a joy in her that would carry her through school, licensure, and leadership.

Carrie

Though Carrie's career trajectory looked linear from the outside, a distinct clarity came early when she worked with at-risk youth. That experience didn't just inform her—it defined her approach to the work. Her passion was born not in theory but in practice, as she witnessed the impact of trust, presence, and structure on the lives of vulnerable young people.

Ruth

Ruth's story began with a compromise. In the 1970s, facing societal pressures and limited options, she opted for a criminal justice degree instead of law school. But what began as a default choice became a transformative path. Social work didn't knock loudly—it slipped in through the back door. Over time, addiction treatment chose her, and what began as circumstance became deep commitment. In retrospect, that unexpected pivot became her true path.

Kathy

Though Kathy began her studies in education, it was Fordham University's Jesuit mission—"men and women for others"—that shifted her vision. Immersed in cultural service programs from Nashville to Alaska, she saw community needs up close and realized that education alone wasn't enough. What she craved was deeper engagement—walking alongside others in their struggle, listening, and facilitating growth. That shift marked the beginning of her life in social work.

Chapter 3: Personal Struggles as Fuel for Purpose

Introduction:

Pain, when integrated, becomes a source of wisdom. The clinicians in this chapter transformed their personal challenges — loss, trauma, adversity — into the very heart of their work. Their stories reveal how suffering can be a bridge to empathy, turning wounds into pathways of healing for themselves and others.

From hardship to healing, these stories show how personal adversity becomes the foundation for deep empathy and professional transformation.

In the crucible of personal struggle, many clinicians discover their most enduring source of empathy. Pain — when acknowledged and transformed — can become the very soil from which purpose grows. In this chapter, we hear from those who faced loss, upheaval, adversity, and identity challenges, and who turned those very experiences into insight, compassion, and a powerful drive to serve.

Jay

Jay's path to becoming a clinician wasn't shaped solely by academic ambition — it was forged in the fire of personal loss. Amid the dissolution of his first marriage and the emotional turmoil that accompanied it, he remained deeply committed to his clinical training. Rather than derailing him, these life changes became a source of insight and deepened his understanding of the complexity of healing and human relationships.

Olivia

Behind Olivia's graceful exterior as a dancer was a woman grappling with her own internal struggles. Years in therapy helped her unpack childhood trauma and emotional blocks. Her injury may have ended her dance career, but it offered an entryway to profound inner transformation. Through confronting her own pain, Olivia found her life's purpose: helping others find their way through the dark, just as she had.

Grace

Grace's story is marked by both personal resilience and professional depth. As a twin, she suffered the unimaginable loss of her brother just before they were to enter college together. Defying her parents' disapproval of her educational pursuits, she forged ahead with tenacity. That early grief, combined with her clinical work with people facing HIV/AIDS in the early 1990s, taught her how to hold space for suffering—and how to advocate fiercely for the dignity of every person.

Jeanne

Being significantly shorter than her peers gave Jeanne a lasting sense of otherness that she learned to transform into insight. Rather than seeing her stature as a limitation, she recognized its power to help her connect with those who also felt different or unseen. Her personal sensitivity became a professional strength, shaping her into a clinician who meets people with deep understanding and presence.

Vilma

Vilma's journey was layered with responsibilities and personal sacrifice. After two decades as a legal secretary and raising five children, she decided to return to school. Caring for her granddaughters while pursuing her undergraduate and master's degrees required extraordinary resilience. Her early struggle to believe in her own worth was slowly replaced by a clear sense of purpose. The very experiences that might have discouraged others became her source of strength and fuel for her future in social work.

AnnMarie

Starting college at 42 came with a sense of vulnerability for AnnMarie. Lacking agency experience, she often questioned her place in the field. Yet, rather than allowing her doubts to paralyze her, she leaned into her creativity and background in art and teaching. Her late start became a strength— a testament to her determination and a reminder that purpose often ripens with time.

Daniel

Daniel's professional transition from law enforcement to social work was marked by personal reflection. Raised with discipline and structure by Ursuline nuns and steeped in Catholic values, he cultivated compassion alongside rigor. His early experiences in youth sports and mentorship reflected his lifelong attempt to reconcile strength with service. The inner discipline that got him through decades of public service also helped him navigate a vulnerable redefinition of self in midlife.

Lynwana

A family tragedy altered the trajectory of Lynwana's life. When her brother suffered a motorcycle accident that left him quadriplegic, she was thrust into the complex world of long-term care. That intimate exposure to caregiving, advocacy, and resilience deeply shaped her perspective on health and family dynamics. Rather than breaking her, the experience broke her open—to a career rooted in compassion, caregiving, and systemic transformation.

Chapter 4: Role Models and Influences

Introduction:

No one becomes a social worker alone. In this chapter, clinicians honor the teachers, mentors, family members, and guides who helped them see their potential and shaped their values. These stories remind us that leadership often begins with modeling—and that a single person's belief in us can change the trajectory of a lifetime.

Mentors, family members, and community figures who modeled care, justice, and service—lighting the way forward.

No one enters the field of social work alone. Often, the spark of service is first witnessed in someone else—a mentor, teacher, family member, or community leader whose values, actions, and presence planted the possibility of a different kind of life. In this chapter, clinicians honor the role models who reflected back their potential, guided their choices, and embodied the values that now define their own professional paths.

Imee

For Imee, the Center for Family Life in Sunset Park was more than a support organization—it was sacred ground. Founded by Sister Geraldine and Sister Mary Paul, CFL provided a model of compassionate, community-rooted service. These two women didn't just support her—they believed in her before she could believe in herself. Their mentorship turned Imee's early struggles into stepping stones, and their legacy lives on in every life she now touches.

Yokasta

Yokasta, too, credits her professional path to the guidance of Sisters Geraldine and Mary Paul. Arriving in the U.S. from the Dominican Republic, she faced the challenges of language and cultural adaptation. But these mentors saw her potential and helped her channel her faith and resilience into service.

Their influence gave her the confidence to pursue social work—not just as a career, but as a spiritual calling rooted in humility and empowerment.

Margaret

Growing up with a father who was a child psychologist, Margaret had a front-row seat to the world of behavioral care. His example instilled in her a fascination with the inner workings of the mind and a deep respect for helping professions. Though she ultimately chose social work for its versatility and scope, her father's dedication laid the foundation for a lifetime of purposeful inquiry and service.

Steven

Surrounded by mental health professionals—his sister, brother-in-law, stepmother, and others—Steven's environment was rich with therapeutic language, compassion, and insight. Still, it wasn't until a friend affirmed his natural gifts during a late-night conversation that he fully considered stepping into the field himself. The support and guidance of a therapist who knew him well helped crystallize the decision, making the path ahead feel not only possible but inevitable.

Lynwana

Family was central to Lynwana's life and career. Her father, in particular, shaped her sense of duty, faith, and service. His influence guided her not only toward the helping professions but also toward a therapeutic approach grounded in advocacy and familial strength. When her brother's accident challenged her entire family system, it was that early modeling that helped her rise to the occasion and build a career that honors the power of kinship.

Karen S

Karen's family faced adversity, but the kindness and skill of a social worker made a lasting impact. That early example of support—offered when her family most needed it—left a blueprint for what care could look like. It wasn't abstract; it was personal. And it inspired her to do for others what had once been done for her.

Stuart

During his time at Brandeis University, Stuart found himself shaped by the activism, inquiry, and interpersonal exploration of his professors and peers. His experiences in encounter groups and anti-war protests introduced him to a different kind of learning—emotional, embodied, and urgent. These influences later guided him into the field of social work, where systems theory and emotional intelligence could be brought together in meaningful ways.

Michelle

Michelle's education and early internships exposed her to the power of interdisciplinary teams—where each voice contributes to a collective vision of care. During her time at Holliswood Hospital's dual diagnosis unit, she learned the value of shared insight and collaborative service. These early mentors modeled not only technical skill, but also humility and respect—cornerstones of the profession she would grow to love.

Daniel

Raised by Ursuline nuns and shaped by the values of his Catholic school upbringing, Daniel's early role models emphasized discipline, integrity, and compassion. These lessons stayed with him through a 30-year career in law enforcement and ultimately influenced his shift into social work. His mentors didn't just teach him how to lead—they taught him how to care, even in the most structured environments.

Vilma

For Vilma, encouragement came from those who saw her long before she saw herself. A neighbor, a supervisor, and a mentor each played a critical role in her transition from legal secretary to clinician. They not only recognized her gifts—they voiced them, celebrated them, and pushed her to pursue the path that had quietly been waiting for her. Their belief became her momentum.

Chapter 5: Shifts from Other Careers or Fields

Introduction:

For some, social work was not the first path—but it was the truest. These stories speak to the courage it takes to change course and pursue something more meaningful. Whether leaving behind careers in law, dance, education, or healthcare, these clinicians followed the call of purpose, trusting that it's never too late to begin again.

When social work chose them—stories of career pivots driven by insight, opportunity, and a sense of deeper calling.

Not all paths into social work are direct. For many clinicians, the journey began elsewhere—law enforcement, education, the arts, healthcare, or even legal administration. Yet somewhere along the way, a deeper calling revealed itself. These stories remind us that it's never too late to choose a new path, and that what we bring from our former lives can deeply enrich the work we do today. In every transition lies the courage to start again—and to align one's life with purpose.

Olivia

Olivia spent years as a professional dancer, expressing herself through movement and finding success in the performance world. But despite her accomplishments, something inside her remained unfulfilled. When a career-halting injury forced her to pause and reflect, she returned to a long-buried dream: becoming a psychotherapist. The emotional depth she once explored through dance now informs her work as a clinician, where she integrates body-based awareness with psychological insight.

Daniel

A decorated law enforcement officer with three decades of service, Daniel's initial career spanned leadership roles in internal affairs, planning, and medical administration. But after retirement, he felt drawn to a different kind of service—one that addressed the emotional and psychological needs of individuals and communities. Grounded in a lifelong passion for wellness, structure, and discipline, his transition into social work became a natural extension of his desire to serve with both strength and compassion.

Ruth

Ruth originally envisioned herself as a lawyer, but in the 1970s, social norms and personal limitations redirected her into a degree in criminal justice. That shift—initially unintentional—ultimately placed her on the path to social work. When she entered the world of addiction treatment, it wasn't by plan, but by resonance. The work spoke to her, and she answered. Her journey reminds us that sometimes the profession chooses us, long before we choose it.

Sarah

Initially drawn to teaching, Sarah discovered during her undergraduate years that the classroom felt too confined for the kind of impact she wanted to make. A conversation with her advisor revealed social work as a possibility, and something clicked. The field's flexibility, dynamism, and deep human connection aligned more clearly with her gifts and values. What began as a detour became her true path.

Someeka

Someeka began her college education in nursing, believing it was the best way to help people. But the structure didn't feel quite right, and she found herself yearning for more versatility. After a series of academic transitions, her aunt's illness and a powerful encounter with a social worker solidified her next move. She pivoted toward social work, where she found the range, creativity, and relational depth she was seeking.

Vilma

Vilma had a full life—working as a legal secretary and raising five children—before her path shifted. The transition began quietly: a comment from a neighbor, an opening in an adolescent care program, encouragement from a supervisor. Before long, she was back in school, pursuing social work with an energy that surprised even her. Her past became her foundation, and every life she now touches is shaped by the wisdom of her lived experience.

AnnMarie

AnnMarie's background in art and teaching gave her a unique lens on the human experience. But it wasn't until she entered college in her forties that she began formally pursuing psychology and social work. Her eclectic interests—art, language, human behavior—converged in the field of social work, where she found a platform for advocacy and creative care. Her shift was not just professional—it was deeply personal, a reclaiming of her identity and purpose.

Kathy

Kathy started her professional journey in education, but it was Fordham University's emphasis on justice, service, and community engagement that expanded her vision. Immersion experiences in marginalized communities revealed a wider field of need—one that required not just teaching but transformation. Social work provided that path, allowing her to blend structure with soul and knowledge with activism.

Grace

Initially drawn to clinical psychology, Grace's early work with individuals living with severe mental illness shifted her path toward social work. The real-world complexity of psychosocial programs—and the relationships she built within them—showed her that healing was less about diagnoses and more about dignity, connection, and creativity. Social work, with its flexibility and human-centered focus, offered the depth she was seeking.

Steven

Though not formally in the helping professions, Steven's early life was surrounded by mental health practitioners. Still, it took a moment of personal insight and external validation for him to shift toward clinical work. His background in writing, communication, and observation became powerful tools in his transition, and his career now bridges the intuitive wisdom of his past with the clinical depth of his present.

Carrie

Carrie's career evolved across various social service settings—beginning with at-risk youth, then domestic violence work, and foster care. Though all her roles fell under the umbrella of care, it was only over time that her professional identity as a social worker solidified. Her shift wasn't abrupt—it was an evolution of purpose. Each transition added layers to her understanding of systems, trauma, and transformation.

Section 1

Part 2

Chapter 6: Early Inspirations and Life Events

The formative moments and early life circumstances that awakened a commitment to service.

Behind every social worker is a story—often one marked not just by a desire to help, but by lived experiences that shaped their earliest understanding of care, justice, and resilience. In this chapter, we meet clinicians whose foundational years—whether spent translating for their families, navigating poverty, or witnessing community inequities—quietly cultivated the values that now define their work. These beginnings didn't always announce themselves as destiny, but in hindsight, they reveal a clear trajectory toward service.

Lisa Marie

Raised in Syracuse, New York, by a single mother grappling with chronic illness, Lisa Marie grew up facing the realities of poverty. "I was the child of a social worker's caseload," she reflects. Her early life was shaped by the kindness of key figures—a compassionate social worker, a dedicated teacher, and a supportive college professor—who saw her potential when she struggled to see it herself. Carrying food packages home from school, she learned what it meant to care for others and survive with dignity. These formative experiences lit a quiet fire in her: to one day be for others what those helpers were for her.

Agnes

As a teenager, Agnes was already showing up for her community—working in after-school programs, summer camps, and as an impromptu translator for neighbors navigating unfamiliar systems. Growing up in a household marked by alcoholism and emotional volatility, she developed empathy not just as a virtue, but as a necessity. These early roles in advocacy and care planted the seeds for a lifelong mission: to help bridge gaps, empower families, and walk alongside those in pain with clarity and compassion.

Cheryl

Cheryl's roots in service trace back to her church community, where a centenarian named Miss Ginter taught her one of life's most enduring lessons: true help is about empowerment, not enabling. This early mentoring gave Cheryl a lens through which to view care—not as charity, but as partnership. Her family's values and the spiritual strength of her community offered a firm foundation for the work she would one day do as a social worker committed to dignity and independence.

Deirdra

Growing up in Harlem's Grant Housing Projects, Deirdra couldn't help but notice the stark divide between her neighborhood and the academic world of Columbia University, just a few blocks away. That invisible boundary—separating opportunity from oppression—fueled her curiosity from a young age. Why do some flourish while others remain stuck? Her desire to answer that question, to bridge the chasm between communities and systems, became the beginning of her life's work.

Guillermina

Guillermina's introduction to the field came not through textbooks but through direct service. Working as a family worker in the Bronx, she accompanied social workers on home visits, supporting families impacted by domestic violence and substance abuse. While still an undergraduate student at Lehman College, she realized that her work wasn't just a job—it was a calling. The early exposure to human struggle and resilience gave her both the courage and the conviction to become a social worker herself.

Sunita

Even as a young girl, Sunita was drawn to people in pain. Looking back, she recognizes that this desire to heal others mirrored a need within herself. Growing up with sensitivity and an instinct for comfort, she knew early on that her life would be spent easing suffering. Her academic journey may have taken longer than expected, but the foundation was always clear: help others the way she once needed to be helped.

Joy-Hee

Arriving in the U.S. from South Korea at the age of 32, Joy-Hee dedicated herself to supporting her husband's academic pursuits and raising their children. For years, she put her own dreams on hold. But throughout her life, she found herself acting as an informal advocate for fellow immigrants—translating, guiding, and connecting people with systems that often excluded them. These lived experiences, deeply rooted in service and community, eventually led her to claim her own path and pursue social work at the age of 52.

Chapter 7: Moments of Clarity or Calling

Pivotal turning points and revelations that confirmed the path to social work.

There are moments in life when everything sharpens—when uncertainty gives way to clarity, and purpose steps into view. For the clinicians in this chapter, such moments appeared in many forms: a conversation, a class, an internship, a spiritual realization, or a surprising job offer. What they all have in common is a sense of alignment—of finding themselves doing the very work they were meant to do. These turning points didn't always arrive with fanfare, but their impact was undeniable.

Lisa Marie

After years in the restaurant industry and no formal training in the helping professions, Lisa applied on a whim for a case management role at the Salvation Army. She was hired—and everything changed. Her first assignment was working with pregnant and parenting teenagers, and what she felt surprised even her: joy. "I just fell in love with social work," she recalls. That unexpected position wasn't just a job; it was a doorway into a life of meaning, purpose, and community impact.

Agnes

Agnes had originally envisioned herself as a bilingual teacher, but something shifted as she began working with veterans during her undergraduate years. It was there, in the trenches of support work, that she felt the spark. She could see the need—and she knew, without question, that she had the capacity to meet it. That click of recognition guided her to pursue graduate study in social work and changed the trajectory of her career.

Devorah

For Devorah, clarity came from struggle. Her recovery from an eating disorder and her spiritual belief that "God didn't give me this for no reason" gave her life new direction. But that clarity didn't come easily—she had no college degree and little financial support. What she did have was purpose. That vision carried her through multiple degrees and into a field where her pain became a pathway to healing for others. Her calling wasn't born in comfort—it was forged through transformation.

Emmanuel

Emmanuel describes himself as an "accidental social worker." While studying law and philosophy in Washington State, he took a Marxist philosophy course that introduced him to a social work classmate. Through conversations with her, he was drawn to the possibility of work that was not only intellectually engaging but socially impactful. Later, while seeking employment in New York City, he landed a job with the Human Resources Administration and felt, for the first time, that he was making a real difference. A career he hadn't even considered had suddenly become his purpose.

Ines

Ines's journey began in a biomedical program, but her soul wasn't in it. A shift to sociology and a class on social work changed everything. When a classmate shared news of being accepted into a social work program, something stirred in her. With every internship—from nursing homes to dialysis units— she felt more aligned, more at home. The clarity didn't come in a flash, but through a series of small confirmations, each leading her closer to her path.

Karen F

Karen's transition from paralegal to child welfare investigator marked a defining moment. While her initial career was rooted in law, it wasn't until she began working for the Administration for Children's Services (ACS) that she realized: this was her work. The blend of advocacy, protection, and systemic change awakened something in her. Pursuing a Master's in Social Work was not just a strategic move—it was the natural evolution of her calling.

Denise

Denise's first motivation was personal—advocating for her speech-delayed daughter. But as she learned to navigate educational systems and advocate for services, she realized this was a skill she could bring to others. Her work with families impacted by disability and addiction was never part of her original plan, but once she stepped into the field, she never looked back. The more she served, the more she felt at home.

Guillermina

As a family worker supporting court-mandated home visits, Guillermina witnessed social workers navigating the complexities of families, trauma, and systems. Initially in a supportive role, she found herself absorbing everything. And then it clicked—this is what I'm meant to do. As she studied social work formally, each class and each client only reinforced that early flash of recognition.

Sunita

It was during her internships—first in mental health housing and later at the YMCA with children—that Sunita realized the scope and power of social work. Seeing firsthand how early intervention could shift a child's life path, she felt the magnitude of her role. The work was hard. The stories were heavy. But the impact was undeniable. She knew she was exactly where she was meant to be.

Scott

After a career in acting, Scott stumbled across hypnotherapy. One session was enough to awaken something dormant within him. The very next day, he saw an ad for Yeshiva University's MSW program. It felt like a sign—one he chose to follow. Though he had never considered social work before, something in him knew this was the next chapter. And it was.

Paul

Paul began in accounting, but the numbers didn't hold his heart. A quiet tug pulled him toward people, not spreadsheets. A psychology course became a turning point, opening a world where empathy, insight, and transformation took center stage. The more he learned about social work, the more he saw its breadth and power—and the more he knew it was his.

Doug

Doug's journey began in the courtroom, advocating within the bounds of the law. But over time, he realized that legal victories weren't always human victories. Wanting more meaningful connection, he enrolled in NYU's social work program— at night, while still practicing law by day. When he began helping parents reconnect with children after years of separation, he knew: this was where real change happened. And this was where he belonged.

Chapter 8: Personal Struggles as Fuel for Purpose

Stories of transformation through hardship, where pain became the foundation for empathy.

Adversity is often a crucible—burning away illusion and awakening a deeper sense of compassion and purpose. For many social workers, personal struggle was not a detour on the path; it was the path. Whether shaped by poverty, illness, trauma, or systemic barriers, these clinicians turned their lived experiences into the very foundation of their professional lives. They do not serve in spite of their pain—they serve because of it.

Devorah

Devorah's journey began with the mirror. Her battle with anorexia and bulimia nearly consumed her, but she came out the other side with something more than recovery: she found meaning. Her faith in God framed her struggle as purposeful, a tool to guide others through the dark. Add to this the pain of two failed marriages and a deep longing for healthier relationships, and Devorah's mission became clear—help others heal from the wounds she herself had survived.

Lisa Marie

Growing up in poverty, Lisa Marie knew what it was like to rely on the kindness of others. Carrying donated food home from school, watching her mother battle chronic illness, and navigating adolescence under those pressures left a mark. But that mark didn't become a scar—it became a map. Her life now is about giving back, about being to others what someone once was for her.

Agnes

Agnes's childhood was a study in contradiction: community involvement on one side, and an alcoholic father on the other. In that mix of service and suffering, she developed a resilience and empathy that would shape everything that followed. She understands chaos and stubbornness, not from a textbook but from memory. That lived understanding is what now makes her a source of steadiness and support to the families she serves.

Deirdra

Raised by a single mother in Harlem's Grant Housing Projects, Deirdra saw inequality up close. The divide between her block and Columbia University just a few streets away wasn't just physical—it was systemic, historical, and personal. That environment raised hard questions: Why do opportunity and struggle sit side by side? Why do some cross the line and others get left behind? These questions became her mission, driving her to become not just a social worker, but a force for equity and justice.

Denise

Denise didn't plan to become a social worker. But when her young daughter struggled with speech delays and the system failed to provide appropriate support, Denise became an advocate. What started as a personal mission expanded into a professional calling. Going back to school at 37 with three children wasn't easy, but Denise knew that her story—and her daughter's—was not unique. Others needed the advocacy she had fought to learn. Her strength is born of necessity, and her work is built on that foundation.

Joy-Hee

For most of her adult life, Joy-Hee prioritized others—her husband, her children, her community. But when her children left home and she finally turned inward, she faced a startling question: What do I want for myself? Despite fears about returning to school at 52 and studying in a second language, she felt ready. The strength she had shown in quiet ways for years—raising a family, translating for neighbors, managing a business—became the very qualities that now shape her presence as a clinician and advocate.

Dara

Until the age of 16, Dara was functionally illiterate. Diagnosed with dyslexia late, she struggled silently for years—feeling lost in systems that weren't designed for her. But once she found the right support, everything changed. Her discovery of psychology felt like unlocking a hidden room inside herself. That transformation—from voiceless to empowered—now drives her to help others access the same kind of breakthrough. Her life is a testament to the healing power of being seen.

Marisha

Marisha's story is one of extraordinary endurance. After leaving college unsure of her direction, she reentered as a working mother determined to reclaim her dreams. Over 13 years, she completed her undergraduate degree, raised her daughter, and worked full-time. Graduate school followed, as did psychoanalytic training. Her hardship wasn't a hindrance—it was a source of determination. Her clinical work now reflects that deep sense of knowing: healing takes time, presence, and fierce perseverance.

Chapter 9: Role Models and Influences

The teachers, mentors, and community members who modeled the path and inspired action.

Sometimes, a single person believing in us can change everything. Whether it was a social worker, teacher, church elder, or community leader, the clinicians in this chapter were shaped by the people who saw their potential and offered them a glimpse of what service, strength, and compassion could look like. These role models didn't just guide careers—they ignited purpose.

Lisa Marie

Lisa Marie grew up amid hardship, but her journey was forever altered by the presence of a few key figures: a social worker, a schoolteacher, and a college professor. They were more than helpers—they were lifelines. Each one saw something in her, named it, nurtured it. Their belief became her bridge, allowing her to imagine a life beyond survival. Today, Lisa channels their legacy in every client she affirms, every student she supports.

Deirdra

In high school, Deirdra met a mentor who helped her see past the limitations of her environment. That relationship was more than educational—it was transformational. Her mentor guided her through the complexities of navigating higher education as a young Black woman from Harlem, and later supported her in accessing programs like Columbia's Double Discovery. Through that mentorship, Deirdra learned that advocacy begins with being seen—and that visibility can be revolutionary.

Cheryl

One of Cheryl's most influential mentors was a centenarian named Miss Ginter. With wisdom grounded in lived experience, Miss Ginter taught Cheryl that true care is not about rescuing—it's about empowering. "She wasn't about enabling people to be weak," Cheryl recalls, "but about enabling them to be strong and independent." This philosophy became a cornerstone of Cheryl's practice, reminding her that every act of service should uplift, not diminish.

Ines

Ines credits much of her early development in social work to her church community, where she became deeply involved in outreach and community-building efforts. These early experiences shaped her view of service—not as a job, but as a way of life. Her faith community modeled connection, mutual support, and advocacy long before she studied them in school. The inspiration she found there still informs her approach to working with diverse and often underserved populations.

Chapter 10: Shifts from Other Careers or Fields

Career pivots from law, teaching, acting, business, and more—toward a life of service.

The call to social work does not always come early. For many, it arises after life has already taken them down other roads—some paved with ambition, others with survival. The clinicians in this chapter began their professional lives in fields as diverse as law, acting, education, and administration. But eventually, something deeper called. Whether through burnout, boredom, or a sense of unfulfilled purpose, they all reached a turning point—and chose service. These stories remind us that there is no wrong path, only a question of when we decide to follow the truth of who we are.

Kathy

"I didn't get into social work to be a clinician," Kathy admits. With a background in administration and a passion for systemic change, she was drawn to the field for its flexibility. Social work, she says, offered her the chance to be an advocate, a leader, and a change agent. Her previous experience gave her perspective—but social work gave her purpose.

Lisa Marie

Before she ever stepped into a case management role, Lisa Marie was working in the restaurant industry, trying to make ends meet. She wasn't looking for a new career—just a job. But her unexpected hire at the Salvation Army shifted everything. Social work didn't feel like work; it felt like home. Her background in hospitality taught her resilience and people skills—tools she now uses every day in therapeutic and advocacy roles.

Agnes

Agnes began her educational journey intending to become a bilingual teacher. But once she started working with veterans and families in need, she knew she wanted something different. The classroom was too narrow; the world of social work was wide open. Her pivot came from a realization that she didn't just want to teach—she wanted to walk alongside people through their hardest moments.

Devorah

Devorah's early adult life was not centered around career—it was about survival. Without a college degree and with little financial support, she had to build her path from the ground up. But her recovery journey, her spiritual reflections, and her experience navigating unhealthy relationships lit a fire in her. Her career shift wasn't just professional—it was personal, spiritual, and hard-won.

Emmanuel

With graduate studies in both law and philosophy, Emmanuel didn't set out to become a social worker. But a chance conversation in a Marxist philosophy class, and a practical job with the Human Resources Administration in NYC, revealed a different kind of fulfillment. What began as an academic detour became a lifelong commitment to people, systems, and transformation.

Ines

Ines started in biomedical studies, then moved to sociology, and eventually into social work. Her detour wasn't a failure—it was a course correction. Along the way, she discovered her passion for community-based care and advocacy. What she thought would be a medical path transformed into a relational one—where healing happened not in labs, but in lives.

Karen F

Karen's career began in law. As a paralegal in New York City's Law Department, she imagined a future in the court-room. But once she transferred to the Administration for Children's Services and began investigating child abuse cases, something shifted. The work felt urgent, impactful, and real. Social work became her new mission—and Columbia University became the launchpad for the next phase of her career.

Denise

Denise's pivot wasn't from a career, but from motherhood. Her advocacy for her daughter's speech therapy sparked a desire to help other families navigate similar challenges. As she shifted from being a mother seeking answers to a social worker providing them, she found a new kind of fulfillment. Her path evolved from necessity—but grew into vocation.

Scott

From stage lights to therapy rooms, Scott's transition from acting to social work was both surprising and intuitive. Acting taught him how to access emotion, connect with character, and use presence—skills that became foundational in his clinical practice. A spontaneous session in hypnotherapy lit the match. The next day, he enrolled in an MSW program. His shift wasn't just a change in career—it was a homecoming.

Paul

Paul started as an accounting major, but something never quite fit. Drawn toward people rather than spreadsheets, he shifted into psychology and philosophy. That change led him to social work, where he found the intellectual depth and inter-personal meaning he had been seeking. His early interest in psychodynamic theory now underpins a clinical approach that honors complexity, trauma, and healing.

Doug

Doug practiced law for years, but the work left him unfulfilled. While helping companies solve problems, he found himself yearning to help people solve them. Enrolling at NYU's School of Social Work, he attended classes at night while still practicing during the day. When he began reuniting families and supporting parents in recovery, he knew he had finally found what he'd been looking for.

Dara

Originally drawn to acting, Dara's journey was shaped by a late diagnosis of dyslexia that changed her entire trajectory. Once she learned to read at 16, she discovered a hunger for psychology and emotional truth that far exceeded the scripts she used to memorize. Her shift to social work wasn't just professional—it was about using her voice to help others find theirs.

Marisha

Marisha left college early, unsure of her path. Years later—after marriage, motherhood, and a cross-country move—she returned with fierce purpose. She earned her degree one course at a time while raising her daughter and working full-time. The pivot to social work required everything she had. But in it, she found everything she needed: structure, purpose, and a place to make real impact.

Closing Reflection: The Call to Serve

Across two parts and dozens of voices, one truth echoes clearly: no two paths into social work are the same—but each one is deeply personal, profoundly human, and fueled by purpose. For some, the journey began in childhood; for others, it emerged through loss, mentorship, or a courageous career shift. What unites them all is the decision to step into the lives of others with compassion, curiosity, and commitment. These stories are more than origin tales; they are reminders of what it means to choose service again and again—and to let lived experience become the heartbeat of healing.

Section 2: Specific Experiences of the Clinician

The Journey – Turning Points, Challenges, and Triumphs

Part I

Chapter 11: First Case or Memorable Clients

Michelle

In her role as Clinical Coordinator at the Renfrew Center of Long Island, Michelle vividly recalls working with a young woman struggling deeply with anxiety, depression, and a diminished sense of self. This client had difficulty expressing herself, her voice barely rising above a whisper during their first session. But over time, through Michelle's compassionate guidance, this woman began to reclaim her voice—both figuratively and literally. With growing confidence, she began speaking up in group sessions, advocating for her needs, and challenging her self-limiting beliefs. Witnessing this transformation reinforced Michelle's commitment to helping women discover their inner strength. "It's not just about managing symptoms," she reflects. "It's about helping people reconnect with who they really are."

Jenna

Jenna remembers Jesus—not as a client, but as a constant presence in her life, even years after their official sessions ended. Jesus was unhoused and living with HIV. He carried layers of trauma and distrust, but also a deep desire to belong. Jenna met him where he was, practicing harm reduction and unconditional acceptance. Over time, Jesus opened up. He shared his story, his dreams, and his fears. The bond they formed went beyond traditional care—it became a relationship rooted in humanity. Jenna credits Jesus with shaping her entire philosophy of service: that healing begins not with fixing, but with listening.

Alishka

A decade spent at Bellevue's Child Protection and Development Center gave Alishka many unforgettable stories, but one child remains etched in her heart. A six-year-old girl who had been removed from her home after surviving severe abuse. She came to sessions angry, shut down, and fearful. Through art therapy and consistent nurturing, the child gradually began to engage. One day, she drew a picture of herself smiling, with the word "safe" scrawled above it. "That moment," Alishka says, "was proof that healing is possible—even after unimaginable harm."

Margaret

Margaret recalls a young man she worked with at the Massachusetts Society for the Prevention of Cruelty to Children. He had witnessed extreme violence in his home and was acting out at school. Teachers and caseworkers had all but given up on him. But Margaret saw past the behaviors to the pain. She visited him regularly at home, spoke with his caregivers, and helped him access therapeutic services. Slowly, he began to open up. He started drawing again, and even talked about wanting to become a teacher. "We need to believe in our clients before they believe in themselves," Margaret says. "That belief can save a life."

Lydia

In her early days at the Center for Alternative Sentencing and Employment Services, Lydia worked with a teenager recently released from juvenile detention. He had been labeled as "dangerous" and "a lost cause." But Lydia saw something different. She noticed how he looked out for the younger boys in the group sessions, how he showed up on time, even when he said he didn't care. With persistence, humor, and consistency, Lydia built trust. The young man eventually completed the program and found employment. Years later, he returned to thank her. "You were the first person who didn't see me as a criminal," he said.

Chapter 12: Stories of Resilience and Healing

Lorie

Lorie's journey in mental health care is itself a story of resilience. Having personally experienced mental health struggles, she now stands as living proof that healing is not only possible, but probable—with the right support and determination. "I went from breakdown to breakthrough," she shares. Her lived experience transformed her therapeutic approach, infusing it with deep empathy. Clients often feel seen in her presence, not just because of her clinical knowledge, but because they know she truly understands. Her life stands as a quiet revolution—showing that healing professionals can be wounded healers and icons of hope.

Carrie

When Carrie made the difficult decision to leave a toxic work environment, it was a leap into the unknown. She channeled her pain into purpose, launching a therapeutic writing business rooted in her belief in healing through expression. Her clients, many of whom felt voiceless or trapped, found liberation through writing. One woman, who had been in therapy for years with little progress, told Carrie, "Writing with you was the first time I felt free." Carrie's resilience became a catalyst for others. Today, as a Training Manager, she continues to inspire transformation—not just in clients, but in fellow clinicians, too.

Jose

Jose's story of resilience is interwoven with his cultural identity. Navigating the challenges of being a Dominican immigrant in the U.S., he initially struggled to feel understood within the mental health field. Rather than becoming discouraged, he turned his challenge into an opportunity. He founded Southern

Dutchess Behavioral Health Services—a clinic that now employs 22 clinicians from diverse backgrounds. His journey reminds us that resilience is not only about surviving adversity, but about transforming systems to be more just and inclusive. "Healing is easier when people feel seen and heard," he says. "That starts with representation."

Ann-Elizabeth

For five decades, Ann-Elizabeth has supported others through their pain—all while managing her own. Living with chronic illness, she could have retreated, but instead she refined her practice to fit her needs, maintaining a private practice for over 30 years. This adaptation wasn't a compromise— it became a strength. Her clients received focused, deeply individualized care from someone who knew how to navigate uncertainty with grace. Her personal struggle cultivated a clinical presence that was gentle, wise, and steady. "Resilience," she reflects, "is not just bouncing back. Sometimes it's about building a new path altogether."

Adaiah

Adaiah's story is one of quiet, sustained strength. Over two decades at Narco Freedom and Samaritan Daytop Village, she walked alongside parents battling addiction, families in crisis, and children navigating chaos. Her strength came not from grand gestures, but from unwavering consistency. "I just kept showing up," she says. Clients learned to trust her because she didn't flinch at their darkest moments. She embraced growth through continuing education, integrated evidence-based therapies, and never lost sight of her north star: authentic human connection. Today, as she prepares to open her private practice, her story continues—rooted in compassion, resilience, and renewal.

Chapter 13: Ethical Dilemmas and Integrity in Action

DonnaSue

Early in her work with homeless individuals living with mental illness, DonnaSue was faced with a moral dilemma. She was instructed to discharge a client for non-compliance with a program rule, though doing so would render him homeless once again. Instead of blindly following policy, she advocated fiercely—offering a different plan rooted in clinical judgment and human dignity. "I couldn't do it," she said. "Ethics must trump policy when policy lacks compassion." Her decision ultimately led to a revision of the agency's discharge process, reinforcing her belief that integrity means challenging the system when it threatens the well-being of those it's meant to serve.

Lydia

Lydia's ethical courage emerged during her work with justice-involved youth. She encountered a situation where a supervisor discouraged her from advocating for a young man's educational rights, fearing it might complicate agency relationships. Lydia stood her ground, aligning her actions with her code of ethics, not bureaucratic convenience. "He deserved a chance," she said. "I didn't become a social worker to stay quiet." The young man later graduated, sending Lydia a note that read, "Thank you for fighting for me when no one else would." Her integrity sparked a ripple of change—not just for him, but for the system around him.

Margaret

When funding for Medicaid-based health home programs came under threat, Margaret faced a dilemma: comply with new restrictions that prioritized numbers over care—or speak out. Choosing the latter, she gathered data, stories, and a coalition of voices to advocate at the state level. It would have been easier to remain silent, but Margaret knew that doing so would betray the very people the system was supposed to serve. "Social work without advocacy is just paperwork," she said. Her stand protected services for hundreds of clients, reinforcing the vital role of ethical resistance in clinical practice.

Monique

As a nurse and social worker, Monique often stood at the intersection of medical compliance and client-centered care. During her time working with incarcerated men, she was asked to fast-track a discharge plan that she knew would put a man with severe mental illness back on the streets without support. Refusing to compromise her values, she fought for an extension—and won. The man later enrolled in supportive housing. Monique's commitment to ethical care, even under pressure, illuminated her core belief: "Our job isn't to tick boxes—it's to protect lives."

Jenna

In her role as Chief Program Officer, Jenna was often caught between administrative expectations and frontline realities. Once, when pressured to cut funding for a harm reduction program that was seen as "not evidence-based enough," Jenna refused. "Evidence," she said, "includes lived experience." Her decision saved the program and ensured continued access to life-saving services for homeless LGBTQ+ youth. Jenna's ethical compass wasn't guided by politics or optics— it was grounded in deep respect for human dignity and the transformative potential of radical acceptance.

Chapter 14: Moments of Doubt and Breakthrough

Carrie

Carrie's moment of doubt came at a crossroads—working in a toxic job that stifled her creativity, undermined her confidence, and left her questioning whether she still belonged in the field. She feared she had failed herself. But rather than abandon her calling, she reached inward—and toward the SWEET Institute. With support and validation, she left her job, launched a therapeutic writing business, and later stepped into a senior role. What had once felt like failure became her greatest breakthrough. "My breakdown," she reflects, "was just a breakthrough in disguise."

Ann-Elizabeth

For Ann-Elizabeth, chronic illness was her constant companion and greatest challenge. At one point, her health became so unpredictable that she considered leaving clinical work altogether. "I feared I couldn't serve my clients the way they deserved," she said. But instead of stepping back, she adapted—shifting into private practice and transforming limitation into strength. This decision not only preserved her career but deepened her empathy. "My clients don't just see a clinician," she shared. "They see someone who knows what it means to struggle—and still choose to show up."

Daniel

Introduced to the concept of "learn, unlearn, and relearn," Daniel initially felt disoriented. It challenged everything he thought he knew—about himself, his work, and the systems around him. But this disruption became his breakthrough. By unlearning rigid mindsets and relearning how to approach change, Daniel emerged more aligned with his mission. "I was no longer just doing therapy," he realized. "I was embodying transformation." What began as confusion became clarity—an invitation to evolve.

Michelle

In her early work, Michelle was often told to "stick to the treatment plan," even when it didn't align with what her clients truly needed. At one point, she questioned whether she was truly helping. Her breakthrough came when she learned to trust her clinical intuition, speak up, and advocate for an inter-disciplinary, client-centered approach. "When I began to see my clients as more than diagnoses—and helped them do the same—everything changed." It was no longer about protocols. It was about people.

Marsha

Balancing motherhood and mental health work, Marsha often wondered if she was enough. Enough for her children. Enough for her clients. Enough for herself. The guilt ran deep—until she reframed the question. "Maybe it wasn't about being everything to everyone," she said. "Maybe it was about being present, where I am." In that moment, she stopped striving for perfection and began practicing compassion—for herself and for those she served. That shift became the foundation of her ongoing work and her own healing.

Chapter 15: Cultural, Structural, and Systemic Challenges

Jose

For Jose, navigating his dual identity as a Dominican immigrant and a mental health professional in the U.S. was both deeply personal and professionally defining. Early in his career, he encountered cultural barriers—both within himself and in the systems around him. "I felt split between two worlds," he shared. Through personal therapy and self-reflection, he began to see this duality not as a conflict but as a bridge. He founded a clinic that embraced cultural inclusivity, staffed by clinicians from diverse backgrounds. "Healing begins when people feel seen," he says. And he made sure they were.

Lydia

When Lydia moved from Canada and the Cayman Islands to New York City, the contrast in pace, culture, and expectations was jarring. She worked in the justice system, helping individuals find alternatives to incarceration, but often felt the system was set up to punish rather than support. She returned home to the Cayman Islands, disheartened yet wiser. There, she redirected her energy to child protection and foster care—applying what she learned in New York to a context where cultural sensitivity and community healing were paramount. "The system taught me what not to do," she said. "Now I can create something better."

Margaret

Margaret's decades in social work brought her face to face with systemic inequities—especially when it came to Medicaid-funded programs. Time and again, she saw programs defunded or devalued, even when they worked. Her response? Advocacy. She built coalitions, documented client success stories, and demanded attention to social determinants of health. "Our clients are not numbers. They're human beings whose lives are transformed by these services," she declared. Her refusal to be silent made her not just a clinician, but a voice for systemic change.

DonnaSue

As a pioneer in New Jersey's first supportive housing program for homeless individuals with mental illness, DonnaSue faced skepticism and systemic resistance. "They didn't know what to do with me," she recalls. With little funding and even less support, she often used her own resources—buying clients coffee and donuts to build rapport. But the greater challenge came in her advocacy for LGBTQ+ older adults. In a system not built to see them, she refused invisibility. "No one should age without dignity," she said. Her work became a lighthouse for a population long overlooked.

Jenna

Working within the social services system, Jenna constantly confronted bureaucratic red tape and funding limitations that often stood in direct contrast to her values. As Chief Program Officer, she refused to let the system dictate the level of care. She championed harm reduction in environments steeped in stigma, creating sanctuary where others saw risk. "Systems can strip people of their agency," she said. "Our job is to give it back." Her work reminds us that healing requires not just compassion—but confrontation with injustice.

Section 2
Part 2

Chapter 16: The Journey – Unique Moments That Shaped Their Path

Karen S: From Foster Care to Systems Leadership

Karen's professional journey began at Wayne State University, where she earned her bachelor's and master's degrees in social work. Her early experiences in child welfare laid a foundation for a career deeply rooted in family reunification and systems change. As psychiatric hospitals in Michigan closed in the 1980s, Karen adapted by leading day programs for older adults. She continued expanding her influence through outpatient programs, substance use treatment initiatives for seniors, and HIV/AIDS services. Her leadership roles in managed care and utilization management reflected her understanding of the intersection between clinical and financial dimensions of care. Even after a cancer diagnosis in 2021 prompted her semi-retirement, Karen continued serving her community through remote private practice and teaching—proof of a lifelong commitment to resilience, innovation, and impact.

Ruth: Leading with Reluctance, Transforming with Purpose

Ruth's foray into social work began with a candid acknowledgment: she didn't choose social work—social work chose her. After earning a master's in criminal justice, Ruth initially worked in substance abuse counseling, frustrated by the cyclical nature of addiction. A pivotal conversation with her supervisor, Hilda Cruz, redirected her path toward social work. At VIP Community Services, Ruth flourished. She became the director of both women's and men's residences and eventually served as assistant vice president of supportive programs. Ruth's legacy includes groundbreaking work with transgender women and a steadfast belief in community empowerment.

Her story is one of embracing one's purpose, even when it reveals itself unexpectedly.

Someeka: From Perfectionism to Wholeness

Someeka's journey was shaped by disillusionment and discovery. After working in unfulfilling jobs, she pursued an MSW from Fordham, driven by a desire to support vulnerable populations. From fee-for-service therapy to crisis work in shelters and hospitals, Someeka experienced both the limits of bureaucracy and the freedom of private practice. Her wellness model—rooted in emotional, social, physical, and spiritual dimensions—was born from her personal battle with perfectionism. A defining moment came during a child welfare case where she filed an Article 10 petition to protect a child from harm. That moment affirmed her commitment to advocacy and safety, transforming her career into one of courage, purpose, and authenticity.

Yokasta: Advocacy Across Communities and Classrooms

Yokasta's career began in the heart of Red Hook, Brooklyn, where she worked in community-based school programs through Good Shepherd Services. Her advocacy for vulnerable children continued in Staten Island and later through the Department of Education. With specialized work in Applied Behavior Analysis (ABA), she built trusting relationships within the autistic community, offering support that was both professional and deeply personal. Now, she champions students with special needs, leads IEP meetings, and introduces restorative practices in the classroom. Her work is a reminder that advocacy can live not only in agencies and clinics but in the everyday rhythms of a school day.

Grace: A Life in Crisis and Connection

Grace's professional identity is defined by intensity and impact. From managing Assertive Community Treatment (ACT) teams to working in supportive housing for individuals with HIV/AIDS and severe mental illness, she has always thrived where the stakes are highest. Her love for crisis work is matched only by her deep mentorship of colleagues and her unwavering advocacy for clients. Now working in a federally qualified health center, Grace continues her mission amidst the structural challenges of the healthcare system. Her story is a testament to adaptability, grit, and the unwavering belief that healing begins with dignity and connection.

Jeanne: Holding Space with Perspective and Grace

Jeanne's path through mental health care has been rich with variation and shaped by personal introspection. She has worked with individuals with dual diagnoses, children with special needs, and adults navigating complex trauma. Through personal challenges—including internalized beliefs about her physical appearance—Jeanne learned to embrace her strengths and let go of environments that didn't celebrate her. A difficult experience at Catholic Community Services taught her to distinguish between self-worth and systemic dysfunction. Known for her balanced outlook and openness to multiple perspectives, Jeanne exemplifies the strength that comes from embracing complexity, both within and around us.

Sarah: Empowerment Through Equity and Education

Sarah's career began with Big Brothers Big Sisters and evolved into a powerful force for systemic change. Her early work highlighted racial and educational disparities, igniting a commitment to culturally competent care. From group homes and high schools to clinical settings and consultation work, Sarah has made it her mission to empower youth and families through trauma-informed practices. After relocating to Maryland and facing the hurdles of re-establishing her clinical career, she founded her own private practice. Her work now bridges direct service, consultation, and mentorship. Sarah's journey is a masterclass in transformation: creating ripple effects by aligning passion with purpose.

Vilma: The Fight to Keep Families Whole

Vilma's unwavering belief in family reunification is at the heart of her work. From her time at the New York Foundling to her current work at Inwood Community Services, she has fought for mothers navigating addiction, trauma, and systemic scrutiny. Her advocacy has led to extended services, systemic reforms, and reunified families. At the same time, she critiques stagnation in the system—clients stuck for decades in services that don't promote independence. Vilma's voice challenges complacency and pushes for holistic, empowering care. Her philosophy is simple but profound: "Children belong with their moms," and with the right support, healing is always within reach.

Stuart Aaronson: Advocacy, Then and Now

Stuart's career spans advocacy, research, and progressive action. As Executive Director of the Runaway and Homeless Youth Advocacy Project, he lobbied for young people in crisis. Later, at Harlem Hospital, he led a grant-based program for families affected by HIV and AIDS, applying his research background to evaluate outcomes and expand impact. Now retired, Stuart remains deeply engaged in political and environmental activism, working with Neighbors for a Greener Harlem and WE ACT. From clinical work to climate justice, Stuart's life reflects a commitment to healing not just individuals but entire communities through collective action.

Steven: Reframing Recovery, One Habit at a Time

Steven's professional identity was forged through firsthand experiences with addiction treatment. His internships across inpatient, outpatient, and long-term rehab settings shaped his understanding of recovery. In Brownsville, Brooklyn, as the first social worker hired in a justice-aligned program, Steven tackled stigma head-on—advocating for smoking cessation as part of recovery. His "Tobacco/Nicotine Awareness" initiative reframed resistance into reflection, helping clients understand relapse risks. Steven's eclectic therapeutic style blends CBT, psychoanalysis, DBT, and EMDR. Today, he continues his work through telehealth, proving that even in virtual space, deep and lasting transformation is possible.

Chapter 17: Stories of Resilience and Healing

In the ever-evolving landscape of mental health care, resilience is more than a buzzword—it is the essence of transformation. For these clinicians, healing has not been a linear journey; it has been a daily act of courage and reinvention. Their stories illuminate how personal hardships and professional challenges have been transformed into opportunities for growth, advocacy, and genuine care. Through setbacks, systemic obstacles, and moments of deep vulnerability, they have discovered the power of empathy and the strength to forge new paths for themselves and their clients.

Karen S: Rising Through Adversity

Karen's career is defined by her ability to adapt and lead. From her early days as a foster care worker to her roles in managed care and emergency settings, she met every challenge with determination. Even after a gallbladder cancer diagnosis in 2021, she embraced a new chapter—engaging in remote private practice and mentoring the next generation of social workers. Karen's resilience is reflected in her unwavering commitment to family reunification and systemic innovation, proving that even when life's trials threaten to slow us down, they can also propel us forward.

Ruth: Transforming Reluctance into Advocacy

Ruth's journey began with a moment of candid self-recognition. Initially a counselor in substance abuse treatment, she was perplexed by the cyclical struggles of her clients. A life-changing conversation with her supervisor, Hilda Cruz, redirected her path toward social work. Rising through the ranks at VIP Community Services, Ruth embraced leadership with compassion—pioneering inclusive practices that expanded services to marginalized groups, including transgender women. Her story is a testament to how personal doubt can evolve into a powerful drive for systemic change, ensuring that no client is left behind.

Someeka: Healing Through Authenticity

For Someeka, the path to healing was paved by acknowledging her own imperfections. After a series of unfulfilling roles, she pursued an MSW and discovered a passion for helping vulnerable populations. Transitioning from fee-for-service therapy to a fulfilling private practice, she developed a holistic wellness model that addresses not only emotional and mental health but also the social, financial, and spiritual dimensions of life. Someeka's defining moment—advocating for a child harmed by domestic violence—cemented her belief in the transformative power of advocacy. Her journey is one of learning to embrace imperfection and using it as a bridge to genuine, client-centered healing.

Yokasta: Bridging Communities with Compassion

Yokasta's professional life has been a study in adaptability and cultural sensitivity. Beginning her career in community-based programs in Brooklyn, she later transitioned into the public education system on Staten Island, where her work focused on supporting vulnerable children and families. Confronted with the challenges of navigating different cultural contexts, Yokasta's resilience shone through as she forged deep, trusting relationships with those she served. Her commitment to restorative practices and individualized advocacy has allowed her to create safe, empowering spaces—reminding us that healing often starts by meeting people exactly where they are.

Grace: A Beacon in Crisis

Grace's work in high-risk environments speaks to a unique blend of passion and resilience. Managing an Assertive Community Treatment team in New York, she thrived in the fast-paced, unpredictable world of crisis intervention. Whether in supportive housing or hospital emergency settings, Grace has consistently provided compassionate, innovative care to those facing severe mental illness and homelessness. Her leadership in mentoring new clinicians further amplifies her impact, proving that true healing can spark from even the most chaotic circumstances.

Jeanne: Embracing Complexity with an Open Heart

For Jeanne, personal challenges became a source of strength. Navigating her own struggles with self-image and feeling different, she learned to harness her uniqueness as an asset. A transformative experience at Catholic Community Services—where she was forced to confront the limits of conventional therapy—taught her that not every setback is personal. Jeanne's ability to view situations from multiple perspectives has allowed her to adapt her practice to meet the diverse needs of her clients, embodying a resilience that is as much about self-acceptance as it is about professional excellence.

Sarah: Empowering Change Through Persistence

Sarah's career is marked by her relentless commitment to equity. Beginning with her work as a case manager at Big Brothers Big Sisters, she witnessed firsthand the disparities affecting marginalized youth. The challenges of starting anew in Maryland, combined with systemic obstacles in educational and clinical settings, spurred her to forge her own path. Founding her private practice became not only a personal breakthrough but also a means to empower the next generation. Sarah's story reminds us that true healing often emerges from the courage to embrace change and to continuously reinvent one's professional identity.

Vilma: The Unyielding Fight for Family Unity

Vilma's work is a passionate crusade against the forces that tear families apart. Whether serving as a substance abuse counselor or as a fee-for-service therapist, she has consistently championed the idea that with the right support, families can overcome even the most daunting challenges. Her advocacy for extended homemaking services and her unwavering belief that "children belong with their moms" have transformed lives and shifted systemic approaches. Vilma's journey is defined by her ability to confront and challenge institutional inertia, driving holistic change with empathy and fierce determination.

Stuart: From Grassroots to Global Impact

Stuart's professional evolution is a story of sustained advocacy and transformation. Beginning as the Executive Director of a youth advocacy project, he tirelessly lobbied for runaway and homeless youth. His later work at Harlem Hospital, where he led a project for families affected by HIV and AIDS, combined rigorous research with heartfelt care. Now actively engaged in environmental and political activism, Stuart continues to channel his deep-seated commitment to justice into every facet of his life. His journey underscores that healing can be both individual and collective—an ongoing process that spans personal, clinical, and societal realms.

Steven: Innovative Approaches to Addiction Recovery

Steven has redefined what it means to support recovery. His early internships in substance use treatment, followed by a groundbreaking role in a Brownsville program, shaped his distinctive approach. Faced with a clientele largely composed of formerly incarcerated individuals, Steven pioneered programs that integrated smoking cessation—reframed as "Tobacco/Nicotine Awareness"—with traditional therapy. His ability to blend cognitive-behavioral techniques with psychoanalytic insight has helped countless clients understand not only how to change their behavior but why they became the way they are. His journey in telehealth further illustrates that innovation and resilience go hand in hand, proving that even in the most challenging environments, healing is possible when creativity meets commitment.

Chapter 18: Ethical Dilemmas and Integrity in Action

In the intricate realm of social work, practitioners often encounter situations where ethical principles conflict, requiring them to navigate complex dilemmas with discernment and integrity. These moments test their commitment to the profession's core values, such as respect for persons, social justice, and professional integrity. The following narratives illuminate how several clinicians confronted ethical challenges, demonstrating unwavering dedication to ethical practice and the well-being of their clients.

Karen S: Balancing Confidentiality and Duty to Warn

Karen's extensive experience in child welfare and mental health services often placed her at the crossroads of confidentiality and the imperative to protect vulnerable individuals. In one instance, while directing a family growth and development center, she encountered a situation where a parent's disclosures suggested a potential risk to their child. Karen grappled with the ethical dilemma of maintaining client confidentiality versus her duty to warn and protect. Drawing upon the National Association of Social Workers (NASW) Code of Ethics, which emphasizes the importance of client well-being and safety, she navigated this challenge by consulting with colleagues and legal counsel to ensure that her actions upheld both ethical standards and legal obligations. Her approach underscored the delicate balance social workers must maintain between respecting client privacy and ensuring the safety of others.

Ruth: Upholding Cultural Competence Amid Personal Beliefs

Ruth's leadership at VIP Community Services involved advocating for diverse populations, including the pioneering inclusion of transgender women in treatment programs. This endeavor required her to confront and reconcile personal beliefs with the ethical mandate for cultural competence and respect for all clients. The NASW Code of Ethics calls for social workers to understand and respect the diverse backgrounds of their clients, promoting social justice and dignity. Ruth's commitment to these principles led her to implement staff training on cultural competence, ensuring that the organization's services were inclusive and affirming. Her actions highlighted the ethical responsibility to provide equitable services to all individuals, regardless of gender identity or expression.

Someeka: Navigating Self-Determination Versus Protection

In her role with the Administration for Children's Services (ACS), Someeka faced the ethical tension between honoring a client's right to self-determination and the need to protect vulnerable individuals. She encountered a case where a parent's choices posed potential harm to their child, challenging her to balance respect for the parent's autonomy with her duty to safeguard the child's welfare. The NASW Code of Ethics acknowledges such dilemmas, emphasizing the importance of professional judgment in determining when to intervene. Someeka approached this situation by engaging the parent in a collaborative dialogue, exploring alternative solutions that respected the parent's autonomy while prioritizing the child's safety. Her thoughtful navigation of this complex scenario exemplified the ethical deliberation required in social work practice.

Yokasta: Managing Dual Relationships in Close-Knit Communities

Working within school systems and community programs, Yokasta often encountered dual relationships, where professional and personal connections intersected. In tight-knit communities, such overlaps are sometimes unavoidable, presenting ethical challenges related to boundaries and objectivity. The NASW Code of Ethics advises social workers to avoid conflicts of interest and maintain clear professional boundaries. Yokasta addressed these dilemmas by establishing transparent communication with clients and community members, setting clear boundaries, and seeking supervision when necessary. Her proactive measures ensured that her professional judgment remained impartial, safeguarding the integrity of her practice and the trust of those she served.

Grace: Allocating Limited Resources Ethically

As a manager of an Assertive Community Treatment (ACT) team, Grace was often confronted with the challenge of allocating scarce resources among clients with severe mental illnesses. Deciding who would receive immediate services and who might have to wait posed significant ethical questions about fairness and equity. The NASW Code of Ethics emphasizes social workers' responsibility to promote social justice and ensure that services are distributed equitably. Grace tackled this dilemma by implementing a transparent triage system based on clinical urgency, ensuring that decisions were made consistently and justly. She also advocated for additional resources to better meet client needs, demonstrating her commitment to ethical practice and systemic improvement.

Jeanne: Confronting Ethical Misconduct

During her tenure at a mental health clinic, Jeanne became aware of a colleague engaging in unethical behavior that compromised client care. Faced with the difficult decision of whether to report the misconduct, she reflected on the NASW Code of Ethics, which mandates that social workers take appropriate action against unethical practices. Jeanne chose to address the issue directly with her colleague, encouraging self-correction. When the behavior persisted, she reported it to the appropriate supervisory channels, prioritizing client well-being and upholding the profession's ethical standards. Her actions reinforced the importance of integrity and accountability in social work.

Sarah: Balancing Personal and Professional Boundaries

In her private practice, Sarah encountered situations where clients sought relationships that blurred professional boundaries, such as connecting on social media or offering gifts. The NASW Code of Ethics advises social workers to maintain clear boundaries to prevent conflicts of interest and preserve the therapeutic relationship. Sarah addressed these situations by educating clients about the importance of professional boundaries, kindly declining gifts, and refraining from engaging in dual relationships. Her adherence to ethical guidelines ensured the integrity of her practice and the trust of her clients.

Vilma: Advocating Within Systemic Constraints

Vilma's work in preventive services and substance abuse counseling often placed her at odds with systemic policies that she believed were not in the best interest of her clients. She faced ethical dilemmas when agency regulations conflicted with her professional judgment about what constituted appropriate care. The NASW Code of Ethics encourages social workers to advocate for changes in policy and legislation to improve social conditions. Vilma approached these challenges by voicing her concerns to agency leadership, proposing policy revisions, and, when necessary, seeking external advocacy channels to support her clients' needs. Her unwavering commitment highlighted the ethical imperative to challenge unjust systems and promote client well-being.

Stuart: Navigating Political Advocacy and Professional Neutrality

Stuart's involvement in political activism alongside his social work practice presented ethical considerations regarding the intersection of personal beliefs and professional responsibilities. The NASW Code of Stuart Aaronson: Navigating Political Advocacy and Professional Integrity

Stuart's career has been deeply intertwined with political activism, reflecting his commitment to social justice and systemic change. Engaging in activities such as canvassing for political causes and participating in peaceful demonstrations, he has been a vocal advocate for marginalized communities. The NASW Code of Ethics acknowledges the importance of social and political action, stating that social workers should engage in efforts to ensure equal access to resources and opportunities, and to advocate for policy and legislative changes that improve social conditions and promote social justice.

While the Code encourages social workers to be aware of the impact of the political arena on practice and to advocate for changes that improve social conditions, it does not prescribe specific causes or activities, allowing practitioners to choose actions aligned with their expertise and passions. Stuart's dedication to political advocacy exemplifies the ethical standard of promoting social justice, demonstrating how social workers can actively contribute to societal change while upholding the profession's core values.

These narratives underscore the complex ethical landscapes that social workers navigate daily. By adhering to the NASW Code of Ethics and engaging in reflective practice, these professionals exemplify integrity in action, ensuring that their decisions honor the dignity and well-being of the individuals and communities they serve.

Chapter 19: Moments of Doubt and Breakthrough

In the intricate tapestry of mental health practice, clinicians often encounter moments that test their resolve and challenge their perceptions. These instances of doubt, however, frequently pave the way for profound breakthroughs, both personally and professionally. This chapter delves into the transformative experiences of several clinicians, highlighting how they navigated uncertainties to emerge with renewed clarity and purpose.

Karen: Embracing Change Amidst Uncertainty

Karen's journey in social work has been marked by a series of transitions, each accompanied by its own set of doubts. From her initial roles in child welfare to supervisory positions, she often questioned her ability to effect meaningful change within bureaucratic systems. The closure of psychiatric hospitals in the 1980s presented another challenge, as she grappled with the influx of patients into community settings. Yet, it was during these periods of uncertainty that Karen discovered her capacity for innovation, developing programs that addressed the evolving needs of her community. Her resilience culminated in her decision to engage in remote private practice following a cancer diagnosis, turning a personal health crisis into an opportunity to continue her life's work in a new format.

Ruth: Confronting Personal Biases

Ruth's entry into the realm of social work was not without hesitation. Initially working as a counselor in substance abuse treatment, she found herself frustrated by the recurring relapses of her clients. A pivotal conversation with her supervisor challenged her to reflect on her own biases and expectations. This introspection led Ruth to pursue a degree in social work, where she learned to approach her clients with greater empathy and understanding. Her subsequent work at VIP Community Services, particularly with marginalized populations, stands as a testament to the breakthroughs that can occur when one confronts and addresses personal doubts.

Someeka: Balancing Professional Aspirations and Personal Well-being

Someeka's path was characterized by a series of roles that left her feeling unfulfilled and questioning her career choices. Her tenure as a senior social worker in a hospital setting, while educational, highlighted the tension between administrative demands and patient care. The constant pressure led her to reevaluate her professional trajectory, ultimately inspiring her to establish a private practice. This move allowed Someeka to develop a holistic wellness model, integrating therapies that resonated with her personal philosophy and addressing the multifaceted needs of her clients. Her journey underscores the importance of aligning one's work with personal values to achieve professional satisfaction.

Yokasta: Navigating Cultural Complexities

Yokasta's career in social work brought her face-to-face with the challenges of serving diverse communities. Transitioning from Brooklyn to Staten Island, she encountered cultural dynamics that often left her questioning her effectiveness. By immersing herself in the communities she served and embracing restorative practices, Yokasta fostered trust and understanding. Her dedication to individualized advocacy and the implementation of therapeutic tools like restorative circles exemplifies how embracing cultural complexities can lead to innovative and effective interventions.

Grace: Rediscovering Passion in Crisis Work

Grace's extensive experience in mental health exposed her to the stark realities of severe mental illness and homelessness. Managing an Assertive Community Treatment team was both exhilarating and exhausting, leading her to moments of doubt about her capacity to continue in such high-stakes environments. However, these challenges prompted Grace to delve deeper into crisis work, where she found renewed passion and a sense of purpose. Her ability to thrive in fast-paced, high-risk situations highlights the potential for personal growth when one leans into, rather than away from, professional challenges.

Jeanne: Overcoming Self-Perception Challenges

Jeanne's personal journey of grappling with self-image issues influenced her professional interactions and confidence. Early in her career, she often felt overshadowed by her own insecurities, which occasionally led to misinterpretations of workplace dynamics. A turning point came when she was unexpectedly dismissed from a position, an experience that forced her to differentiate between personal shortcomings and organizational changes. This realization empowered Jeanne to embrace her unique qualities, enhancing her therapeutic relationships and reinforcing the value of self-acceptance in professional settings.

Sarah: Bridging Administrative Roles and Clinical Passion

Sarah's ascent into administrative positions provided her with a broad perspective on systemic issues within mental health services. However, the distance from direct client interaction led to feelings of disconnect and doubt about her career direction. Recognizing her yearning for hands-on engagement, Sarah transitioned back into clinical work, eventually establishing her own practice. This shift not only rekindled her passion but also allowed her to integrate her administrative insights into creating more effective and compassionate client services.

Vilma: Championing Family Reunification

Vilma's dedication to keeping families intact often placed her at odds with systemic structures that favored separation in cases of substance abuse. Her unwavering belief in the potential for parental rehabilitation was met with skepticism, leading her to question her stance. Through persistent advocacy and witnessing successful reunifications, Vilma's convictions were validated, reinforcing the importance of steadfastness in the face of professional doubt.

Stuart: Integrating Activism with Clinical Practice

Stuart's involvement in political activism occasionally clashed with his roles within structured organizations, causing him to question the compatibility of his advocacy with his professional responsibilities. By finding avenues to merge his passion for social justice with his clinical work, such as leading projects for families affected by HIV/AIDS, Stuart achieved a harmonious integration of his values and vocation. His experience illustrates the potential for creating meaningful change when personal convictions are aligned with professional endeavors.

Steven: Innovating in Addiction Treatment

Steven's work with mandated clients in substance use treatment exposed him to the challenges of addressing co-occurring addictions, particularly nicotine dependence. His initial efforts to introduce smoking cessation programs were met with resistance, leading him to question the feasibility of such initiatives. By reframing the conversation and emphasizing the connection between smoking and relapse, Steven successfully implemented educational programs that resonated with clients, showcasing the power of adaptive strategies in overcoming professional obstacles.

These narratives collectively underscore the transformative potential inherent in moments of doubt. By confronting uncertainties head

Chapter 20: Embracing Change and Innovation

In the dynamic field of mental health, embracing change and fostering innovation are essential for growth and effective practice. This chapter explores the journeys of clinicians who have navigated shifts in their careers, adapted to new methodologies, and pioneered innovative approaches to better serve their clients.

Karen S: Innovating in Managed Care

Karen's transition into managed care and quality assurance marked a significant shift in her career. As a clinical director and later as the director of utilization management, she gained a comprehensive understanding of the intersection between clinical care and financial management. Her work in hospital emergency rooms further expanded her expertise, allowing her to collaborate closely with medical professionals and address acute psychiatric needs. Karen's ability to integrate clinical insight with administrative acumen exemplifies the innovative spirit required to navigate the complexities of modern healthcare systems.

Ruth: Pioneering Inclusive Practices

At VIP Community Services, Ruth's leadership was instrumental in developing programs that embraced diverse populations, including the groundbreaking inclusion of transgender women. Her commitment to progressive approaches and community empowerment showcases the importance of innovation in creating inclusive and effective mental health services.

Someeka: Developing a Holistic Wellness Model

In her private practice, Someeka focuses on a wellness model encompassing eight dimensions: emotional, social, environmental, financial, occupational, physical, intellectual, and spiritual. By incorporating Cognitive Behavioral Therapy (CBT) and Acceptance and Commitment Therapy (ACT), she assists clients in achieving a balanced life. Someeka's approach highlights the significance of integrating various therapeutic modalities to address the multifaceted nature of well-being.

Yokasta: Implementing Restorative Practices

Within the school system, Yokasta plays a pivotal role in advocating for children with special needs. She navigates the complexities of Individualized Education Program (IEP) meetings with parents, ensuring that each child's educational journey is tailored to their unique requirements. Beyond academics, she introduces restorative circles as a therapeutic tool, creating safe spaces for students with emotional disabilities to express themselves and build crucial social-emotional skills. Yokasta's innovative use of restorative practices underscores the importance of creating supportive environments that foster healing and growth.

Grace: Adapting to Federally Qualified Health Centers

In her current role at a federally qualified health center (FQHC), Grace continues to provide therapy and support, adapting to the unique challenges of the healthcare system while remaining focused on her mission. Her ability to navigate the complexities of FQHCs demonstrates the necessity of flexibility and innovation in delivering quality mental health care within diverse organizational structures.

Jeanne: Embracing an Eclectic Caseload

Jeanne's career path has been anything but linear, reflecting her adaptability and openness to new experiences. From working with individuals with dual diagnoses of physical disabilities and mental health challenges to supporting children with special needs in schools, Jeanne has embraced a diverse caseload with enthusiasm. Her ability to see multiple points of view and adapt her practice to meet the unique needs of each client exemplifies the innovative mindset required in the ever-evolving field of mental health.

Sarah: Founding a Private Practice

The onset of the pandemic prompted a significant shift in Sarah's career. Facing challenges in her previous roles, she decided to establish her own private practice, allowing her to maintain a larger caseload while providing personalized care. This decision, though initially daunting, reflects her loyalty to her clients and her belief in the transformative power of therapy. Sarah's ability to adapt to the evolving landscape of mental health care is a testament to her resilience and creativity.

Vilma: Advocating for Systemic Change

Vilma has consistently highlighted the traumatic impact of separation on children, advocating for approaches that prioritize unification rather than division. Her resilience and determination have inspired the lives of countless others, demonstrating that, with the right support, healing is possible. Vilma's deep belief in the power of keeping families together drives her work, emphasizing that, while foster care may be necessary in some situations, the trauma of separation leaves scars that are difficult to heal.

Stuart: Integrating Activism with Clinical Practice

Since his retirement from Harlem Hospital, Stuart has returned to his early passion for progressive political work. He has been actively involved in canvassing for political causes, participating in peaceful demonstrations, and advocating for environmental justice through his work with organizations like WE ACT. His commitment to social justice continues to drive his involvement in causes that affect marginalized communities, particularly those impacted by climate change and systemic inequality. Stuart's integration of activism with clinical practice highlights the role of innovation in addressing broader societal issues through mental health initiatives.

Steven: Innovating in Addiction Treatment

Steven's passion in the field of addiction treatment includes addressing tobacco and nicotine use. In his early internships, he developed programs for clients, including creating presentations to encourage smoking cessation, recognizing that continuing to smoke could dramatically increase their chances of relapsing on more dangerous substances. Steven's innovative approach to integrating smoking cessation into addiction treatment exemplifies the importance of addressing all aspects of a client's well-being.

These narratives collectively underscore the transformative power of embracing change and fostering innovation in mental health practice. By adapting to new challenges and pioneering creative approaches, these clinicians have enhanced their professional growth and significantly improved the lives of those they serve.

Chapter 21: Cultivating Leadership and Mentorship in Mental Health Practice

Leadership and mentorship are foundational elements in the evolution of mental health practice. This chapter delves into the experiences of clinicians who have embraced leadership roles and committed themselves to mentoring the next generation of mental health professionals, thereby fostering a culture of continuous learning and compassionate care.

Karen S: A Legacy of Leadership and Teaching

Karen's journey is marked by her ascent from direct service roles to supervisory and directorial positions, culminating in her tenure as director of a family growth and development center. Her leadership was characterized by a steadfast dedication to family reunification and support for parents navigating the complexities of child welfare. Beyond her administrative roles, Karen extended her influence into academia, teaching at Wayne State University and Phoenix University. Through these positions, she imparted her extensive knowledge and experience to aspiring social workers, emphasizing the integration of theoretical frameworks with practical application. Her commitment to education and mentorship has left an indelible mark on the field, inspiring countless professionals to pursue excellence in their practice.

Ruth: Championing Progressive Leadership

Ruth's career at VIP Community Services is a testament to her progressive leadership and dedication to inclusivity. Starting as a counselor, she ascended to director of both women's and men's residences, and later to assistant vice president of supportive programs. In these roles, Ruth was instrumental in developing and implementing programs that served diverse populations, notably pioneering services for transgender women. Her leadership not only transformed organizational practices but also set new standards for cultural competence and inclusivity in mental health services. By mentoring staff and advocating for marginalized communities, Ruth has fostered an environment where innovation and empathy drive service delivery.

Grace: Guiding Through Crisis and Beyond

Grace's extensive career spans various roles, including managing an Assertive Community Treatment (ACT) team in New York. This position demanded acute crisis intervention skills and provided her with opportunities to mentor a diverse team of social workers and mental health professionals. Her leadership in high-pressure environments has been characterized by a balance of assertiveness and compassion, ensuring that both clients and staff receive the support necessary for growth and healing. Grace's dedication to mentorship has cultivated a cadre of clinicians adept at navigating the complexities of mental health crises with resilience and empathy.

Stuart: Integrating Advocacy into Leadership

Stuart's career trajectory reflects a seamless integration of clinical leadership and social advocacy. As Executive Director of the Runaway and Homeless Youth Advocacy Project, he not only managed organizational operations but also served as a prominent spokesperson and lobbyist for youth in crisis. His leadership extended to Harlem Hospital, where he directed a grant-funded project supporting families affected by HIV and AIDS, emphasizing both program development and rigorous evaluation. Stuart's commitment to mentorship is evident in his efforts to bridge clinical practice with policy advocacy, inspiring emerging professionals to view leadership as a platform for systemic change.

Steven: Innovating Leadership in Addiction Treatment

Steven's ascent in the field of addiction treatment showcases his innovative approach to leadership. Beginning with internships in various substance use treatment settings, he quickly identified gaps in existing programs, particularly concerning smoking cessation. By developing educational presentations and advocating for the integration of tobacco awareness into recovery programs, Steven demonstrated proactive leadership. His roles in organizations like Odyssey House in Harlem further allowed him to implement unique resources that engaged clients more deeply in their recovery journeys. Steven's mentorship of staff and clients alike underscores his belief in empowering individuals through education and self-awareness.

These narratives collectively highlight the transformative impact of leadership and mentorship in mental health practice. By embracing roles that extend beyond direct service, these clinicians have shaped organizational cultures, influenced policy, and nurtured the professional growth of countless individuals. Their stories serve as a testament to the enduring power of guidance, support, and visionary leadership in fostering a more compassionate and effective mental health landscape.

Section II

Part 3

Chapter 22: First Case or Memorable Clients

In every clinician's journey, there are moments that leave a lasting impression—cases that challenge, transform, and ultimately define the trajectory of one's professional path. These memorable clients are not just stories; they are turning points, where theory meets the complex, unpredictable reality of human lives. For the clinicians in this chapter, these moments were more than just milestones—they were mirrors reflecting their own growth, compassion, and commitment to the field.

Sol: The Power of Presence

For Sol, one of her earliest and most memorable cases came during her time at HeartShare, when she was tasked with conducting home studies for prospective adoptive parents. One family, in particular, had endured multiple losses and struggled with infertility. Despite their pain, they remained hopeful and eager to adopt. Sol guided them through the process with care, witnessing not just their external transformation but their internal healing. "It wasn't just about the paperwork," she reflects. "It was about building trust, allowing space for grief, and watching hope take root again." That family eventually adopted a child, and Sol's presence during that journey cemented her belief in the healing potential of relationship-based social work.

Shannon: The Spark of Social-Emotional Learning

For Shannon, every student presents a new opportunity to connect and empower. One particularly memorable student had been labeled disruptive and was frequently suspended. But Shannon saw beyond the behavior. Through weekly SEL lessons, mentoring, and snowboarding sessions with the Chill Program, Shannon watched the student blossom into a leader among peers. "He started to regulate his emotions, help others, and even led a circle," she recalls. "It reminded me why I do this work. We can't give up on kids—especially the ones who seem the hardest to reach."

Imee: When Play Becomes a Lifeline

Working in a middle school, Imee was asked to run a group for LGBTQ+ students. Expecting deep conversations, she instead encountered a group that just wanted to do arts and crafts. "At first, I thought I was doing it wrong," Imee laughs. "But then I realized—they didn't want therapy. They wanted joy." One student, who had previously been bullied, began to look forward to the group every week. "He said it was the only place he could breathe," Imee shares. That moment reshaped her understanding of what therapeutic presence can look like.

Kathy: A Healing Bridge Between Systems

As a program manager for a SAMHSA grant, Kathy remembers a client who had been in and out of psychiatric hospitals for years. He had HIV, untreated hepatitis C, and had long given up on trusting providers. But with integrated care—psychiatry, primary care, and consistent therapy—his life began to change. "He stopped drinking, started managing his medications, and eventually got housing," Kathy shares. "I remember walking with him to his first doctor's appointment and thinking: This is what it means to bridge systems. It's slow, but it saves lives."

Lisa Marie: A Graduation Against All Odds

In a small office tucked inside a high school, Lisa met a student who was barely attending class. She was dealing with trauma, substance use, and an unstable home. Through therapy, yoga, and distress tolerance skills, Lisa supported her for two years. On graduation day, the student handed her a handwritten letter: "You didn't just help me stay in school. You helped me stay alive." Lisa still keeps the letter in her drawer, a reminder of what it means to walk alongside someone in their darkest hours.

Agnes: The Unspoken Pain of Grief

Agnes once worked with a middle-aged woman who had lost her husband, her son, and her home within a span of two years. The client came to her with fibromyalgia and constant emergency room visits. "Others saw her as difficult or manipulative," Agnes recalls. "But I saw pain." Through consistent support, Agnes helped the woman name her grief, connect with spiritual practices, and regain a sense of purpose. "It wasn't just therapy—it was bearing witness to suffering and reminding her she mattered."

Emmanuel: Michael and the Mirror of Potential

Emmanuel met Michael in a transfer school—a place for students who had fallen through the cracks. At first, Michael was defiant, skipping sessions and dismissing therapy. But Emmanuel persisted. Through trust and mentorship, Michael not only graduated but went on to become a real estate broker. "He came back to tell me he was helping people find homes," Emmanuel says. "And I realized—this work plants seeds that grow in unexpected ways."

Ines: The Quiet Bravery of Vulnerability

Ines recalls a client who had been abused and silenced for most of her life. During sessions, she barely spoke. But with time, Ines's gentle presence became a safe container. One day, the client brought a journal and read aloud a poem she had written about reclaiming her voice. "I cried," Ines says. "Not because of the words—but because of the courage it took to share them." That moment reaffirmed Ines's belief in the quiet, transformative power of safe spaces.

Karen F.: Helping Families Begin Again

Karen will never forget the mother she helped through the Beacon Center. Escaping domestic violence, the woman needed not only a new home but a new start. Karen helped her find housing, connected her to community programs, and even assisted in furnishing the apartment. Years later, the mother returned with her teenage son to say thank you. "It wasn't just about case management," Karen reflects. "It was about believing in her when she didn't believe in herself."

Chapter 23: Stories of Resilience and Healing

Resilience often emerges in the quiet moments—in the choice to keep going, to keep believing, and to keep showing up even when the odds are stacked against you. In this chapter, we witness stories of clinicians who not only held space for others' healing but walked through their own trials with grace and courage. Their stories remind us that healing is rarely a single moment; it is a mosaic of small, intentional acts of care—for self and for others.

Sol: Healing Through Integration

Sol's resilience was shaped not only by the demands of her profession but by her lived experiences—raising a child, returning to school, and re-entering a field she deeply loved. After leaving social work for almost a decade to run her family's grocery business and care for her son, she returned with a deeper sense of empathy. The challenges she faced in the Department of Education—learning special education law, managing parents' fears, and advocating within a rigid system—only strengthened her resolve. "I had to grow fast," she says, "but that growth made me a better support to others." Sol's story is one of integration: of life, work, hardship, and healing—woven into a career marked by quiet perseverance and steady hope.

Shannon: Building Systems of Care

For Shannon, resilience is not just personal—it's structural. As the only mental health professional in her school, she often felt the pressure of being the sole responder to complex emotional needs. Yet she chose not to carry the burden alone. She built a system—professional development for teachers, mentoring programs for students, and partnerships with organizations like Burton's Chill Snowboarding. "I wanted to build something sustainable," she says, "so the work continues even when I'm not in the room." Her story is one of turning limitation into innovation, and of building systems that care, even in the absence of traditional support.

Imee: Embracing Difference, Cultivating Belonging

Imee's resilience was born from difference. Diagnosed with a learning challenge in college, she often felt out of place in academic settings. But instead of giving up, she found new ways to learn—eventually channeling her own struggle into her therapeutic work. Her creative, arts-based approach to group therapy became a lifeline for students who, like her, didn't always thrive in traditional spaces. "When people feel seen, they begin to heal," she says. Imee's story is one of transforming self-doubt into connection, using creativity as both a mirror and a bridge to belonging.

Kathy: Leading Through Transition

Kathy's resilience was tested during the era of bail reform, when her program quadrupled in size almost overnight. As team leader, she had to restructure workflows, hire staff, and maintain quality—all while ensuring her team didn't burn out. "It was overwhelming," she admits, "but it taught me the power of adaptability." Even in the face of systemic upheaval, Kathy never lost sight of her clients' humanity. Her leadership—rooted in trauma-informed care and grounded in practicality—allowed her team to navigate the storm without losing their center.

Lisa Marie: A Safe Harbor for Teenagers

Working with high school students facing trauma, Lisa's days are often filled with crisis, heartbreak, and hard conversations. Yet she shows up—with yoga mats, journals, and a belief in every student's potential. When a student once told her, "You're the only person who sees me," Lisa knew her work mattered. Her resilience lies in her consistent presence, her refusal to label or give up, and her use of unconventional tools to unlock healing. "Sometimes all a kid needs is someone who won't flinch," she says. In that steadiness, healing begins.

Agnes: Service as a Sacred Commitment

For Agnes, resilience is intertwined with service. Whether helping victims of domestic violence or starting a food pantry at her church, she has always gone beyond the therapy room to meet people's needs. "It's not just about talking—it's about showing up," she says. Her ability to navigate systems, advocate for Hispanic families, and stay grounded in her faith has carried her through some of the hardest cases. Agnes's healing work flows from a deep well of compassion, rooted in her values and sustained by her unshakable sense of purpose.

Emmanuel: Equity as a Daily Practice

Emmanuel's story of resilience spans decades, shaped by nights of two-hour sleep, multiple jobs, and relentless advocacy. He returned to graduate school later in life, authored training manuals, led family therapy initiatives, and insisted on equity at every table he sat at. Whether reminding physicians to listen to housekeepers or waking up at 5 a.m. to support his staff, Emmanuel modeled a radical kind of resilience—one that refuses to accept injustice and quietly rebuilds systems from within. "Fairness is non-negotiable," he says. "And if I lose comfort to uphold it, so be it."

Ines: Compassion Without Conditions

Ines has weathered both personal and professional storms, often holding space for clients navigating immense grief. She approaches each case with an open heart, even when the behavior is high-risk or the pain runs deep. One client, overwhelmed by chronic illness and repeated ER visits, reminded Ines of the temptation to judge. But she chose compassion instead. "She wasn't attention-seeking—she was seeking relief," Ines says. Her resilience lies in her refusal to close her heart, her belief in non-judgmental care, and her quiet insistence that healing is possible for everyone.

Karen F.: Continuing the Work with Grace

Even after decades in the field, Karen continues to find meaning in small victories—a mother helped, a group started, a client seen. When bereavement counseling became needed for seniors in her current position, Karen didn't wait—she began gathering participants, knowing the impact could be life-changing. "This work doesn't end," she reflects. "It evolves with us." Her resilience is marked not by grand gestures but by consistent, grounded care that ripples through communities and generations.

Chapter 24: Ethical Dilemmas and Integrity in Action

Every clinician, at some point, stands at a crossroads of ethics, faced with choices that test their principles and define their integrity. In the lives of these practitioners, moments of moral challenge have been pivotal. How they responded – with honesty, courage, and a steadfast commitment to do right by their clients – not only protected those in their care but also shaped their own professional identities. This chapter delves into those difficult decisions and the unwavering integrity that guided them.

Karen Felton Handley encountered such dilemmas early and often in child welfare. As a new investigator with the Administration for Children's Services, Karen walked into ethically gray situations regularly. In one notable case, she was assessing a household where cultural practices of discipline bordered uncomfortably on what the law defines as abuse. The parents were recent immigrants, sincerely trying to raise their children well, yet a report had been made about physical punishment. Karen felt the tension between enforcing regulations and respecting cultural context. She could have defaulted to a punitive approach, but her integrity pushed her to dig deeper. She spent extra time speaking with the family in their native language (with an interpreter's help), consulting cultural liaisons, and truly listening. Ultimately, instead of rushing to remove the children, Karen crafted a solution that involved parenting classes and community support, with close monitoring to ensure the children's safety. It was a balancing act: safeguarding the kids while treating the parents fairly and humanely. This decision was not the easiest bureaucratic route, but it was the right one in her eyes – and it worked. The family accepted help without feeling unjustly persecuted, and no further incidents occurred. Karen's integrity in action – prioritizing the children's wellbeing and the family's dignity over a check-the-box approach – demonstrated ethical leadership. She often reflects that "social work isn't black and white; it's many shades of gray, and you need your moral compass every day." That compass guided her to keep families together whenever safely possible, reinforcing the value of compassion in enforcing child welfare laws.

In the sphere of mental health and administration, Emmanuel Charles became known for his principled stands, even when they challenged workplace hierarchy. Throughout his career in hospitals and public agencies, Emmanuel believed in equity – that every team member and every client deserved respect and voice. One situation remains legendary among his colleagues. During a high-level meeting at a psychiatric hospital, junior staff and support personnel were being ignored as decisions were made about patient care protocols. A nurse aide hesitantly raised a concern, only to be talked over by a physician. Sensing the injustice, Emmanuel, who was a program director at the time, calmly interrupted the meeting. He insisted that everyone at the table be heard, explicitly inviting the aide to continue speaking. The room fell silent – it was uncommon for someone in Emmanuel's position to so directly counter a doctor's dominance. After the meeting, a superior scolded Emmanuel privately, suggesting that by flouting hierarchical norms he might harm his career prospects. Emmanuel's response was clear and without anger: principle over promotion. "I'm not seeking a promotion; I'm seeking fairness," he replied. For him, the ethical imperative was creating an environment where the best ideas – and the truth about patient care – could surface, regardless of rank. This stance carried some professional risk, but Emmanuel's consistency earned respect over time. He later developed hospital policies to ensure ancillary staff had channels to provide input, formalizing the inclusive ethos he championed. His actions in those moments of dilemma – whether to stay silent or speak up for justice – revealed an integrity that would not waiver. Emmanuel's commitment to doing right by others, even if inconvenient, became a model for younger clinicians who watched him marry ethical conviction with bold action.

Agnes Timberger often faced subtler ethical challenges in her therapy practice and community work, especially around protecting client autonomy while ensuring safety. Working with survivors of domestic violence, Agnes frequently grappled with the question: How do I respect a client's choices that I might personally disagree with, without compromising their safety? One example was a client who, after months of counseling, was considering returning to an abusive partner – a decision Agnes instinctively wanted to argue against. Every protective fiber in her being screamed to persuade the client to stay away. Yet, Agnes knew that ultimately forcing her will could disempower the client further. So she took a deep breath and leaned into her training and ethics. She helped the client carefully weigh the risks, develop a safety plan, and consider the needs of her children, all without judgment or ultimatums. Agnes made it clear she would continue to support the woman no matter her decision, and that her door was always open. In doing so, Agnes honored the client's right to self-determination, a core social work value, while also fulfilling her duty to warn and protect by discussing the potential dangers and ensuring the client had resources in place. It was a delicate tightrope to walk. In the end, the client decided not to return to the abuser – but crucially, she later told Agnes that it was knowing she had agency and a supportive ally either way that empowered her to make that choice. Agnes's ethical stance – empower rather than coerce – exemplified integrity. Even when her personal feelings tugged one way, she stayed true to the principle that lasting change must be owned by the client. Such moments are emotionally taxing, but Agnes credits her strong supervision and personal reflection for guiding her through. The integrity she maintained in respecting her client's freedom likely saved a life in a way a directive approach might not have.

Within school settings, Shannon Cullen has confronted ethical dilemmas as well, particularly when the interests of her students collided with institutional policies. As the lone social worker in her school, Shannon often found herself advocating for a student against a rule or navigating confidentiality issues. She recalls a scenario with a 15-year-old student who confided in her about suicidal thoughts but begged her not to tell anyone for fear of being hospitalized. Shannon was torn; protecting the student was paramount, yet breaching trust could cause the student to shut down. Demonstrating ethical integrity, Shannon followed protocol to ensure the student's safety – involving a crisis team and the student's parents – but she did so in the most compassionate way possible. She sat with the student through the disclosure, explaining each step of what needed to happen and why, treating him as a partner in the process rather than a problem to be managed. Though it was painful for the student in the moment, that transparency preserved their therapeutic alliance. In the aftermath, Shannon continued to meet with him daily, even visiting him at the hospital as allowed, reinforcing that she hadn't betrayed him but rather was right there with him through it all. Over time, he came to understand that her actions were rooted in care, not punishment. Shannon's colleagues noted how meticulously she balanced ethical duties – to maintain confidentiality and to prevent harm – two values that often clash in school crises. By choosing the path that ultimately safeguarded the student's life while also striving to maintain trust, Shannon showed that integrity isn't just about following rules, but about upholding the spirit of those rules: the well-being of the young person at the center.

Kathy Pierson faced an ethical crucible during the implementation of bail reform in her criminal justice work. When the laws changed and her supervised release program's client load quadrupled virtually overnight, Kathy was caught between administrative pressure to process people like numbers and her ethical commitment to treat each client as a person. There was no roadmap for handling so many cases with the same level of care. She and her team were stretched thin, and the easy route would have been to reduce their services to mere check-ins and court reminders. Instead, Kathy doubled down on integrity in action. She fought for additional staff and lobbied for resources to keep counseling and referral services robust. In team meetings, when asked if they could cut corners to meet quotas, she responded by invoking their mission: "We are here to help people build stability, not just to make sure they show up to court." At times, this stance put her at odds with higher-ups focused on numbers. Kathy had to make hard choices about setting boundaries – like capping caseloads per counselor – and openly communicating to the judiciary that quality might falter if they didn't slow the flood. It was risky to speak truth to power, but ethically necessary to prevent burn-out and neglect of clients. Her frank assessment led to temporary funding for emergency hires and a restructuring that ultimately protected both clients and staff from being lost in the shuffle. Kathy's actions exemplified integrity on a programmatic level: she refused to sacrifice ethical standards of care even under immense systemic pressure. This experience reinforced her belief that social work, whether clinical or administrative, must always circle back to human values. In reflecting on that time, Kathy is proudest not of the metrics they met, but of the fact that "we never treated our clients like statistics." They remained individuals with stories, needs, and rights – and honoring that, for Kathy, is the very essence of ethical practice.

Through these scenarios – in child welfare, mental health, education, criminal justice, and community settings – shines a consistent theme: integrity is the backbone of effective practice. These clinicians often stood in the gap between rigid rules and complex human realities. Their stories show that ethical dilemmas rarely have easy answers; the right course is sometimes the harder one, requiring reflection, consultation, and moral courage. Whether it was Karen choosing family preservation with safeguards, Emmanuel flattening a hierarchy to give everyone a voice, Agnes championing a client's autonomy, Shannon carefully balancing confidentiality and safety, or Kathy challenging a system to preserve dignity – each acted with a deep sense of responsibility and justice. In those critical moments, they were guided by empathy and an unwavering commitment to core values: respect for persons, fairness, beneficence, and truth. These decisions not only protected clients and colleagues in immediate ways, but also set a tone of trust and integrity in their organizations. For junior staff watching or clients on the receiving end, such acts send a powerful message that ethics are not abstract codes on a paper – they are living commitments demonstrated through choices every day. The integrity of these clinicians, tested under fire, became a beacon that illuminates their ongoing journey and inspires others in the field to hold themselves to the same high standard, no matter how tough the call.

Chapter 25: Moments of Doubt and Breakthrough

No journey in this field is without periods of doubt – times when even the most seasoned clinician questions their efficacy, their path, or whether they can continue under mounting pressures. Yet it is often in these very moments of uncertainty that the seeds of the next breakthrough are sown. The following stories explore how each clinician faced their inner doubts and emerged with new insights, renewed purpose, and often, profound personal and professional transformation.

Early in her career, Sol Reyes Pelosi found herself at a crossroads of doubt. In the mid-1990s, after several demanding years in foster care, Sol made the difficult decision to step away from social work to help her family's struggling grocery business. As months turned into years, she worried that perhaps she had given up on her calling. There were nights restocking shelves when she wondered, "Is it too late for me to go back? Am I still a social worker at heart, or have I lost that part of myself?" That doubt lingered nearly a decade, even as she gained life experience and maturity. The breakthrough came when an opportunity arose in 1993 to return to the field at HeartShare, a child welfare agency. Nervous but determined, Sol re-entered social work, initially unsure if her skills were still relevant. To her relief, she discovered that her compassion and dedication had only deepened. However, one insecurity remained: she lacked a master's degree in a field where advanced credentials were increasingly expected. This nagged at her confidence. "I felt I needed more knowledge to effectively support my clients," Sol recalls. Finally, she confronted this doubt head-on and enrolled in a Master of Social Work program in 1999 while working full-time and raising her son. It was an overwhelming challenge – juggling papers, night classes, and parenting – and she certainly had moments of fatigue and second-guessing her choices. But graduating in 2001 was Sol's breakthrough moment. She describes earning her MSW as transformative: it was not just a degree, but a testament to her resilience and commitment. Armed with new knowledge and the confidence that she could overcome personal hurdles, Sol found her voice as a leader and advocate. The very doubts she'd had about leaving the field and about her qualifications became fuel driving her to become an even stronger clinician. Today, as she mentors younger social workers, Sol often shares this journey: how stepping away eventually brought her back with greater clarity, and how conquering her self-doubt by furthering her education empowered her to serve with both heart and expertise.

Emmanuel Charles experienced a crisis of doubt in the middle of an otherwise distinguished career. After years of balancing two jobs and even pursuing doctoral studies, Emmanuel hit a wall in the late 1990s. He had embarked on a Ph.D. program with dreams of influencing social policy, but life threw him an ultimatum: his program demanded he finish his dissertation in an unrealistically short timeframe or be forced out due to prolonged enrollment. Exhausted and sleep-deprived from trying to do it all – full-time work, family responsibilities, and doctoral research on traumatic prison experiences – Emmanuel doubted his ability to push any further. Ultimately, he made the painful decision to leave the doctoral program incomplete. This felt like a personal failure. He wondered if he had overestimated himself by trying to reach too high. For a man who prided himself on perseverance, this unresolved goal was a heavy doubt that shadowed him through the following years. He continued his work – retiring from public service and taking on a clinical role at Rikers Island – but in the back of his mind, the unfinished doctorate felt like an open wound or a dream deferred. The breakthrough for Emmanuel came from an unlikely source: community. In retirement, somewhat adrift, he joined the SWEET Institute's learning sessions to stay busy. Surrounded by supportive colleagues and invigorated by new ideas, Emmanuel felt a spark that he thought had died. Encouraged by peers and mentors who believed in his wealth of experience, he dared to revisit his old doubt. In his 50s, when most might shy away from big endeavors, Emmanuel enrolled in a new doctoral program – this time with a clear plan and the backing of a community that cheered him on. The three years of that program were intense, but he was fueled by purpose rather than ego now. He chose a research topic close to his heart (the impact of inclusion policies on often-ignored hospital staff) and poured his lifetime of insight into it. In 2024, when Emmanuel walked across the stage to finally receive his doctorate, it was more than an academic achievement; it was a redemption of his earlier doubt. The standing ovation from his peers and family was symbolic – through doubt, he had found not only a second chance but a deeper understanding of himself. Emmanuel emerged with the wisdom that it's never too late to chase a dream and that sometimes failure in one chapter lays the groundwork for triumph in the next. His journey teaches that breakthroughs can come even after decades, turning what once felt like defeat into a platform for even greater impact.

For Lisa Marie Sokolowski, doubt often crept in as she tried to balance multiple roles and identities. As a young single mother without a college degree, Lisa Marie sometimes questioned whether she was aiming too high by dreaming of a career in social work. Later, as she juggled raising children, working full-time in social services, and attending graduate school, the sheer weight of responsibility led to dark, exhaustion-fueled nights of doubt. There were moments, after tucking her kids into bed and staring at a daunting stack of textbooks, when she thought, "I can't do this all… maybe I should quit something before everything falls apart." One particularly trying period was during her MSW internship: by day she was a social worker in training dealing with emotionally draining cases, by night a waitress to make ends meet, and always a mom around the clock. A turning point came during a conversation with her own social work mentor, who reminded Lisa of her why – why she started on this path. The mentor gently pointed out how Lisa's life experiences, even the current struggles, were shaping her into the kind of compassionate, relatable clinician that clients desperately need. Lisa had a breakthrough in perspective: her doubt – that she wasn't cut out for this – transformed into a realization that her hardships were in fact carving out her unique strength. The very fact that it was hard meant it was worth it. Soon after, she landed a role that combined her practical skills and newfound degree, validating that all those sacrifices were building to something meaningful. Later in her career, whenever caseloads became overwhelming or bureaucracy wore her down, Lisa would recall how far she'd come – from a little girl relying on food pantries to a woman running one, from a struggling student to a licensed therapist. Each personal hurdle overcome became a reservoir of empathy and encouragement she drew upon for her clients. Thus her moments of doubt, rather than defeating her, birthed a resilient confidence: if she could navigate her own storms, she could certainly help others through theirs. Lisa's journey illustrates how breakthroughs are often born from the very doubts that once threatened to derail us. By reframing her struggles as proof of her resilience, she emerged more grounded and sure of her purpose than ever.

In a profession built on hope, even hope's champions can falter. Shannon Cullen had always been a beacon of positivity for her students and colleagues, yet a few years ago she hit a personal low that shook her self-assurance. Despite her successes with innovative programs at her school, Shannon was burning out. Being "the only mental health professional in the building," as she often was, took a toll. She began to question whether her efforts were truly making a difference or if she was just a Band-Aid on a much larger wound in the educational system. The trigger for her doubt was a tragic incident: a former student she had counseled attempted suicide shortly after graduating. Though the young adult survived, Shannon was wracked with guilt and second-guessing – had she missed warning signs, failed to equip him enough? She considered whether all the social-emotional curricula, the mentoring outings, and heartfelt talks ultimately mattered. It was a crisis of faith in her work and in herself. In this vulnerable time, Shannon sought support and did something she always advised her students to do: she talked about it. Through supervision and peer consultation (some of it via the SWEET Institute network she trusted), Shannon allowed herself to express her fears and grief. Rather than diminishing her, this honest reckoning became the seed of a breakthrough. She realized that she had been carrying the weight of her students' outcomes on her shoulders alone – an impossible burden. In embracing her own limits, Shannon paradoxically found a new freedom and clarity. She recommitted to her mission with a healthier mindset: her role was to do her absolute best for each student, but also to acknowledge that outcomes aren't solely hers to control. This renewed perspective led her to push for systemic changes, like securing a grant to hire another counselor and establishing a teacher wellness program so that the whole community could share the responsibility of student well-being. The personal doubt that nearly convinced Shannon to step away instead propelled her to innovate further. She came out of that tough year with deeper humility, yes, but also a stronger support network and smarter self-care practices. Shannon's breakthrough was understanding that asking for help and sharing the load is a strength, not a weakness. With that lesson, she continues her work with even greater compassion – for her students and for herself.

Imee Hernandez's critical moment of doubt occurred surprisingly at a point when things seemed to be aligning well. She had earned her graduate degree and secured a coveted scholarship to work in the public school system – a dream come true, or so it seemed. Then a hiring freeze slammed that door shut. Suddenly, the clear path she had worked so hard for was in limbo, and Imee felt lost and disappointed. She wondered if leaving her initial track (education) for social work had been a mistake, since now even social work wasn't giving her a foothold in the schools. Watching peers move into steady jobs while she pieced together work in various mental health roles, Imee questioned, "Did I choose the wrong path? Will I ever find the right opportunity?" This period of uncertainty stretched for years longer than she anticipated. Yet in hindsight, it was precisely this detour that became her breakthrough. Since she couldn't join the schools immediately, Imee ventured into diverse roles – from case management with adults to community therapy to running creative arts groups for youth. Each experience added a layer to her skill set and confidence. She discovered new passions, like the therapeutic power of creativity, when an assignment had her integrate arts and crafts into counseling for LGBTQ+ teens. By the time the Department of Education lifted the freeze and offered her a position, Imee was far more prepared and versatile than she would have been earlier. She stepped into the school social worker role not as a novice, but as a seasoned clinician with a toolkit full of innovative approaches. The doubt from years prior – the fear of stagnating – had given way to a rich period of professional growth that was, in fact, a blessing in disguise. When Imee finally walked into a school building as an official social worker, she realized how much those side journeys had taught her about meeting people where they are. It was a moment of profound self-validation. The very twist that once felt like failure turned out to be fundamental to her success. Now, whenever a roadblock appears, Imee thinks back to that hiring freeze and remembers that sometimes the direct route isn't the most rewarding. Her faith in the process is stronger, knowing that patience and persistence can turn even the bleakest detours into valuable new directions.

Each narrative in this chapter reveals a powerful insight: doubt is not the end of the story. In fact, for these clinicians, it was often the dark tunnel they traversed to emerge into a brighter, more enlightened stretch of their journey. Their breakthroughs took many forms – an achievement (a degree, a completed goal), a mindset shift, a newfound community of support, or an unexpected career pivot – but all share a quality of transformation. Through facing their doubts, they didn't just return to the status quo; they came through on the other side changed for the better. And in transforming themselves, they gained renewed energy to transform the lives of others. Personal and professional growth are deeply intertwined in these stories. Sol's academic accomplishment bolstered her work with families; Emmanuel's academic redemption amplified his voice for equity; Lisa's reframing of struggle enhanced her empathy; Shannon's vulnerability improved her practice and advocacy; Imee's patience broadened her expertise. These clinicians learned to treat their own doubts much as they treat their clients' struggles – with patience, compassion, and an eye towards the strengths and possibilities hidden within. The message that resonates from their experiences is one of hope and resilience: it's often when we think we have reached a limit that we discover a new path. By walking through doubt with courage and support, these professionals found breakthroughs that not only reaffirmed their purpose, but also enriched the depth and authenticity they bring to their work every day.

Chapter 26: Cultural, Structural, and Systemic Challenges

The field of social work and mental health does not exist in a vacuum; it operates within cultural contexts and large systems that can both enable and hinder the work. Each of these clinicians has confronted broader structural and societal challenges — from navigating bureaucracies and policy changes to bridging cultural divides — as a core part of their practice. In their stories, we see how they became agents of change within systems, and how acknowledging and addressing these bigger forces was essential to truly help their clients. This chapter highlights their experiences grappling with (and often reforming) the cultural, structural, and systemic aspects of their roles.

Karen Felton Handley's career offers a vivid example of innovating within and against structural constraints. In the 1990s, as a new social work graduate, she joined New York City's efforts to overhaul community services by launching Beacon Centers – after-school community hubs placed in public school buildings. Tasked with setting up one of the first Beacon Centers from scratch, Karen quickly learned how challenging systems-change work can be. She had to coordinate with multiple city agencies, a school principal protective of her building, and skeptical neighborhood residents. There were mountains of red tape in hiring staff and securing funding for programs. Yet Karen's vision of a safe, enriching space for youth and families in a high-need community drove her forward. She maneuvered through bureaucracy by building personal relationships – inviting the principal and local leaders to planning meetings, listening to their concerns, and enlisting them as allies. Culturally, she made sure the center's programs (tutoring, sports, family counseling) were tailored to the community's predominantly immigrant population, even hiring bilingual staff. One structural triumph Karen recalls is when she cut through months of administrative delays to get building repairs done by organizing a "community paint day," effectively shaming the city into action by garnering media attention with volunteers ready to improve the space. Over time, the Beacon Center became a model of community collaboration. One of Karen's proudest moments was helping a single mother in the program – who had been homeless – secure a new apartment and furnish it through a network of donors she'd cultivated. It was a small-scale victory with big symbolic value: the system (in this case, housing and welfare services) often made that mother feel invisible, but through Karen's advocacy and the Beacon's resources, the family found stability. Karen often reflects that working "within the system" meant constantly pushing against its inertia and fragmentation. Her career in community programs and later in child welfare management was marked by many such challenges – from adapting to policy swings in welfare reform to addressing structural racism that affected the families she served. By staying adaptable, politically savvy, and rooted in the community's real needs, Karen turned systemic roadblocks into stepping stones. She demonstrated that clinicians can be architects of change, creating new programs and pathways where none existed, and ensuring that large systems bend, however slowly, towards justice and accessibility.

In the clinical trenches, Kathy Pierson routinely faced the interplay of individual needs with systemic failures, especially in healthcare and justice settings. One of the structural challenges she tackled head-on was the siloed nature of healthcare for her mental health clients. Early in her career at a mental health clinic in Brooklyn, Kathy noticed many clients with serious mental illness were also in poor physical health, often not following up with doctors or managing chronic illnesses like diabetes. The system treated mind and body separately, to the detriment of the person. So when a federal grant opportunity arose, Kathy spearheaded a program to integrate primary care into her clinic. This meant convincing a medical provider to work on-site and coordinating with a major hospital.

It was an ambitious structural intervention that required negotiating data-sharing agreements (a bureaucratic nightmare) and training mental health staff to do basic health screenings. But Kathy's persistence paid off. The program identified dozens of clients with untreated hypertension, HIV, and other conditions, and connected them to immediate care right in the familiar clinic setting. She recalls how revolutionary it felt to have a primary care doctor and a psychiatrist collaborating in real time on a client's behalf – something the old system made very rare. Not only did this improve health outcomes, it modeled a more holistic approach that later became a best practice in many agencies. Kathy's work in the criminal justice arena further highlights her engagement with systemic challenges. Implementing the bail reform initiative in New York put her at the forefront of a massive structural shift: moving from a cash bail system to one where many more individuals are released under supervision. The challenge was twofold – cultural (shifting attitudes from punitive to supportive) and structural (scaling up services quickly). Kathy had to educate judges and court officials about the supervised release program's value, essentially advocating for a change in the judicial culture towards seeing defendants as community members in need of support, not just risks. Structurally, she retooled her team's operations to accommodate a much larger volume, creating new intake protocols and community partnerships (for employment, substance abuse treatment, etc.) to handle the flood of referrals. It was systems change on the fly, often messy and overwhelming. Yet Kathy's guiding star was ensuring that amidst a huge policy change, the humanity of each client didn't get lost. Through her efforts, hundreds of people – who formerly would have languished on Rikers Island due to lack of bail – instead received counseling, court reminders, and linkage to services under her program. Many successfully made their court dates and avoided jail altogether, a tangible outcome of structural advocacy. Kathy's story underscores that social workers often act as the bridge between individuals and the labyrinthine systems they must navigate, and that by improving those systems even incrementally, we improve countless lives.

For Emmanuel Charles, confronting systemic and structural challenges became almost a calling within his calling. As a Haitian immigrant and a man of color rising through the ranks of social service agencies, he was acutely aware of how larger systems – be it racism, bureaucracy, or rigid hierarchies – affected both clients and staff. One major structural challenge Emmanuel took on was within the workplace culture itself at a large forensic psychiatric hospital. He noticed that support staff (like ward aides, housekeepers, drivers) – many of whom were also people of color from immigrant backgrounds – were often overlooked in policy discussions and felt alienated by new Diversity, Equity, and Inclusion (DEI) initiatives that seemed superficial. While patients' needs were front and center, the well-being and voices of these essential workers were not. Emmanuel decided to focus his doctoral research on this very issue, essentially using academia as a lever to address a structural blind spot. His research revealed that a significant majority of ancillary staff felt DEI policies did little for them or even had negative effects, highlighting a gap between institutional rhetoric and reality. Presenting these findings to the hospital administration was a bold move – it shed light on uncomfortable truths about the institutional culture. Some in leadership were defensive, but Emmanuel's decades of respected service gave weight to his words. He advocated for concrete changes: including support staff representatives in policy planning, offering professional development and clear pathways for advancement, and cultivating a more inclusive environment where every role is respected. This was systems advocacy from within, aiming to transform the culture of an organization so it better served all its people, staff and clients alike. Moreover, Emmanuel consistently acted on the systemic level through policy involvement. He would often mentor younger social workers to engage with policy, reminding them that decisions in distant offices profoundly shape front-line realities. Whether pressing the city for better home care funding or questioning why certain communities lacked mental health clinics, he brought the voice of practice to policy tables. One particularly impactful example: while at the Human Resources

Administration, he authored a training manual bridging communication between medical professionals and social services. That manual became a required training component, subtly changing how two systems interacted for years to come. Emmanuel's career demonstrates that clinicians can be scholar-activists and policy shapers, not only serving within systems but relentlessly pushing those systems to be more equitable, culturally humble, and responsive. His efforts remind his colleagues that each case exists in a broader context – and improving that context is part of the job.

Ines Mercedes Alcantara has navigated cultural and systemic currents throughout her 30-year career, particularly as a bilingual, bicultural clinician serving largely Latinx clients. A recurring structural challenge for Ines has been the lack of culturally appropriate services for the Spanish-speaking community. Early on, she encountered clients who had been misdiagnosed or misunderstood by providers due to language barriers and cultural miscommunication. Determined to be an agent of change, Ines took on additional roles beyond therapy – she became a sort of informal cultural consultant at her agency, educating colleagues on issues like the nuances of machismo in domestic violence cases or the importance of involving extended family in treatment when appropriate. She also fought for language access: pushing her clinic to hire more bilingual staff and to translate informational materials properly (not just via clunky automated translations). In one instance, a monolingual Spanish-speaking client with lupus and depression had been labeled as "non-compliant" by hospitals because she frequently visited the ER. Ines recognized a systemic issue: the healthcare system wasn't coordinating her care or explaining things in a way she could understand. Ines stepped in to advocate with the hospital, arranging for a case manager who spoke Spanish to help the client manage appointments and understand her medication regimen. It took persistent calls and meetings, but eventually the client's ER visits dropped as her health stabilized under consistent care. This was a victory over a fragmented system that often leaves such patients falling through the cracks. Ines's efforts also extend to connecting clients with resources outside the therapy office, acknowledging that healing often requires tackling structural problems like poverty, lack of housing, or legal status. She has, for example, liaised with domestic violence shelters to secure a bed for a client and her children when the usual protocol would have had them on a waitlist; she has sat on inter-agency task forces addressing how city services fail undocumented immigrants, lending her clients' experiences (anonymously) to advocate for policy adjustments. These are not roles one might expect a psychotherapist to play, but Ines knows that without engaging the larger system, her clients' progress in sessions could be undone by external barriers. By straddling the worlds of clinical practice and systems advocacy, she ensures cultural and structural factors are accounted for in each client's care. Ines likes to say that her job is part therapist, part navigator. Indeed, she navigated her own path as an immigrant professional and now helps others navigate systems not built with them in mind. Her legacy is not only the individuals she has helped directly, but also the gradual shifts in her agency and community that her advocacy has achieved – like the normalization of Spanish-language support groups and the clinic's ongoing partnership with a Hispanic community center. These structural changes will continue to benefit clients for years to come, a ripple effect of Ines's tireless efforts.

Agnes Timberger confronted cultural and systemic barriers both in her community outreach and within the system as a staff member with family responsibilities. She often served as a cultural bridge for immigrant families confused by the American social service and legal systems. For instance, Agnes spent part of her career working with a program assisting victims of domestic and sexual violence. She found that many Hispanic families were wary of engaging with authorities due to fear of deportation or mistrust of government agencies – a systemic issue of accessibility and trust. Agnes took it upon herself to do outreach in churches and local markets where these families frequented, essentially bringing services to them in their comfort zones. She also translated complicated legal procedures into simple Spanish explanations, demystifying the process of getting a restraining order or accessing public benefits. By doing so, Agnes helped dismantle the barriers that kept vulnerable families from seeking help. On a different front, Agnes also navigated structural challenges as an employee when balancing her career with raising a child with autism. Traditionally, human service workplaces weren't always accommodating of employees' family needs – an often unspoken systemic issue of work-life balance in caring professions. Agnes faced moments where inflexible schedules or bureaucratic rules could have forced her to step back from a job she loved. However, thanks to a supportive supervisor (and Agnes's own advocacy for herself), she was able to negotiate flexible hours and remote work days long before such arrangements were mainstream. This not only allowed her to continue contributing professionally, it also subtly paved the way for a more family-friendly perspective in her agency. By proving that productivity could be maintained with accommodations, Agnes helped shift her workplace culture to be more supportive of working parents – a systemic change benefiting others after her. Furthermore, Agnes's embrace of telehealth during the COVID-19 pandemic was another instance of adapting to structural change (in this case, a global one) and finding opportunity. Moving her therapy practice online, she initially worried older clients or those in poverty might not adapt well to video sessions. To her surprise, many thrived with the easier access. Recognizing the potential, Agnes advocated for her agency to invest in lending out tablets and training clients in their use. As a result, individuals who once had trouble attending in-person sessions due to transportation or childcare issues could now get consistent support. This blending of human touch with technology pointed toward a systemic evolution in service delivery, one Agnes was proud to champion. In all these ways, from community trust-building to workplace policy to digital innovation, Agnes's story illustrates that systemic challenges are multifaceted – and so are the strategies to overcome them. Her approach has always been holistic: identify the gap, whether cultural misunderstanding or policy limitation, and then address it through collaboration, creativity, and compassion.

Shannon Cullen and Imee Hernandez likewise engaged with structural challenges in the education system. Shannon's introduction of a comprehensive social-emotional learning curriculum at her charter school was not just a personal project, but a challenge to the typical school culture. She was asking teachers, who were pressed to raise test scores, to devote class time to feelings and relationship skills. Initial resistance was palpable – "We're not counselors, why do we need to do this?" some educators grumbled. Shannon responded by providing user-friendly lesson plans and framing SEL as benefiting academics too (students who can manage emotions learn better). Over several years, this cultural shift took root, and the school saw decreases in behavioral incidents and improved attendance. Shannon essentially engineered a structural change in the school's approach, weaving mental health into the fabric of education. Meanwhile, Imee, in her work with the Department of Education and community organizations, often tackled structural inequities like lack of resources in underfunded schools. In one case, at a middle school, she noticed LGBTQ+ students had no supportive outlet, and bullying was a serious issue. The system had provided a generic anti-bullying assembly once a year, but nothing ongoing. Imee collaborated with the school to start an arts-based support group as a lunchtime club, giving those students a safe space weekly. It was a modest initiative in scale, but for those kids it drastically improved their sense of belonging and safety at school. It also signaled to the school administration the need for more permanent supports, planting the seed for a Gay-Straight Alliance club that formed later. Such efforts show how frontline clinicians like Shannon and Imee don't just provide services; they influence systems (schools, in this case) to be more empathetic and responsive environments for young people.

From these rich experiences, it's clear that addressing cultural, structural, and systemic challenges is not ancillary to clinical work – it is an integral part of it. These clinicians learned that you can pour all your skill and heart into one individual, but if the system around that individual is broken or biased, progress will stall. So they became advocates, educators, and innovators: Karen building new community structures, Kathy integrating and reforming services, Emmanuel championing equity and policy change, Ines ensuring cultural competence and access, Agnes bridging community and institution, Shannon and Imee reshaping school environments. Each did so in different ways, but all with a shared strategy: never accept "that's just how it is". Instead, they asked, "How can we make it better?" and then rolled up their sleeves to collaborate on solutions. In doing so, they not only helped their own clients, but also many unseen others who will benefit from the changes they set in motion.

Their stories teach us that cultural humility, persistence in the face of bureaucracy, and courage to challenge the status quo are as crucial as empathy and listening skills. They remind us that social issues like poverty, racism, and inadequate public policy often lie at the root of personal struggles – and that healing and justice demand work at both the individual and systemic level. By engaging with big-picture challenges, these clinicians keep the "person-in-environment" perspective at the forefront, striving not just to help the person cope with a difficult environment, but to help change the environment itself. It is complex, never-ending work, often frustrating, yet immensely rewarding when a system bends, even slightly, toward fairness or a cultural gap closes with understanding. In those moments, the structural barriers that once seemed immovable reveal themselves as breakable, and hope extends beyond one client to a whole community or workforce. Through their dedication, these professionals have illuminated a path for all of us in the helping fields: to see every challenge, no matter how daunting, as an invitation to improve the world that our clients live in, not just their immediate circumstances.

Closing Reflections

Each chapter of this section has woven together the voices and experiences of Sol, Shannon, Imee, Kathy, Lisa Marie, Agnes, Emmanuel, Ines, and Karen, highlighting the multifaceted reality of clinical work. Through first cases and memorable clients, we saw the spark that ignited their passion. In stories of resilience and healing, we witnessed the triumph of the human spirit and the reciprocal growth of client and clinician. Ethical dilemmas tested their principles, only to reinforce their integrity and commitment. Moments of doubt opened the door to breakthroughs, leading to deeper self-awareness and renewed purpose. And in facing cultural, structural, and systemic challenges, we learned how these clinicians became advocates and change-makers beyond the therapy room. Throughout, a consistent tone of authenticity, empathy, and strength shines through – these are real people in the helping profession, leveraging their humanity as much as their training. Their narratives illustrate that personal and professional transformation is a continuous, intertwined journey. As they empower others, they are themselves transformed by each lesson learned and each obstacle overcome. Taken together, the experiences of these nine clinicians form a rich tapestry of what it truly means to serve: it means to listen deeply, act with courage and compassion, grow from adversity, and never lose sight of the strengths within every individual and every community. In sharing their journeys, they honor the distinct contributions each has made, while creating a cohesive story of hope and dedication. Their collective wisdom invites all of us – whether seasoned practitioners or new to the field – to reflect on our own pivotal experiences and to carry forward a legacy of learning, integrity, and heart in the work we do. In the end, the specific experiences of the clinician are as diverse as the clinicians themselves, yet they converge on a universal truth: by helping to heal others, we inevitably heal and evolve ourselves, and this mutual growth is one of the profound gifts of the profession.

Section II

Part 4

Chapter 27: First Case or Memorable Clients

In the beginning of every clinician's journey, there are clients whose stories become etched into memory—marking a turning point, awakening a deeper understanding, or sparking a transformation within. These are the encounters that stay with us long after the sessions end. They are not always about perfect resolutions; sometimes they are about the questions we learn to live with, or the courage we witness in another. In this chapter, clinicians reflect on the clients and early experiences that shaped their path and defined what it meant to serve.

Paul: Baptism by Fire

Fresh out of graduate school and just 25 years old, Paul found himself facilitating group counseling sessions for HIV-positive individuals experiencing homelessness and addiction—many recently released from incarceration. The early 1990s was a time of great stigma and fear surrounding HIV and AIDS, and Paul was thrown into the heart of it. "They looked at me like, 'Who the heck are you to help me?'" he recalled. Yet this challenge forged resilience. Moderating those intense sessions not only gave Paul firsthand experience with raw human suffering, but also taught him humility, authenticity, and the importance of simply showing up with respect and consistency.

Sunita: Eyes Lifted, A Heart Reclaimed

One of Sunita's most powerful early clients was a woman who entered therapy unable to make eye contact, burdened by years of emotional abuse and a shattered sense of self-worth. Over time, with gentle encouragement and trauma-informed care, the woman began to reconnect with herself. "She started smiling. She took pride in herself. She even set boundaries with her family," Sunita shared. That transformation—from victimhood to empowerment—remains one of Sunita's most treasured reminders of the healing power of presence and patience.

Guillermina: The Young Mother and the Dialysis Machine

In the pediatric unit of a hospital, Guillermina worked with a teenage mother whose infant required peritoneal dialysis. It was not just the complexity of the medical condition, but the emotional toll on the mother and family that made this case unforgettable. Guillermina navigated discharge planning, crisis counseling, and cross-disciplinary coordination—all while witnessing the unspoken grief of a young mother trying to stay strong. "I saw how social work can be the anchor," she said, "when everything else is shifting."

Scott: Holding Space When No One Else Would

Scott spent over a decade working with individuals affected by HIV/AIDS and substance use, many of whom lived on society's margins. One early case that stayed with him was a client who had been chronically ignored and dismissed by other systems. "He told me, 'You're the first person who listened to me without making me feel like trash.'" That moment cemented Scott's commitment to creating spaces where clients could feel safe, seen, and valued—regardless of their background or circumstances.

Joy-Hee: Healing in a Second Language

Visiting families in their homes early in her career, Joy-Hee remembers one mother who had fled domestic violence and was trying to rebuild a life in a country where she didn't speak the language. Joy-Hee, herself an immigrant, could communicate in Korean, bridging a critical gap. "Sometimes, just speaking someone's language is healing," she reflected. It was a moment that crystallized her understanding of cultural connection and the invisible wounds of displacement and survival.

Doug: Finding Purpose in Caregiving

While supporting his father through a terminal illness, Doug realized that his personal experience was informing his professional calling. He began volunteering with older adults, and one client—a man in his eighties battling depression after losing his wife—remains vivid in his mind. "He taught me that grief doesn't follow a timeline, and neither should care," Doug said. The client eventually found solace in community and purpose, and Doug found his path in geriatric social work.

Dara: The Girl Who Didn't Fit the System

One of Dara's early clients was a teenage girl with pervasive developmental disorder who had been bounced from one program to another. Frustrated by the lack of fit, Dara helped create an entirely new initiative—REACH—that recognized and responded to the unique needs of this population. "She wasn't the problem," Dara said. "The system was." That case became the catalyst for Dara's career in building programs where others saw only gaps.

Deirdra: The Mothers Behind the Statistics

While working in supportive housing for women experiencing homelessness and serious mental illness, Deirdra was moved by the strength and vulnerability of one mother in particular. "She had lost everything, yet was determined to rebuild her life for her children," Deirdra recalled. That case shifted her understanding of social work from task completion to relational depth—seeing people not as problems to solve, but as lives to honor.

Denise: Layers of Pain, and the Path Out

In the early 2000s, Denise met a man cycling through hospitalization, jail, and shelters—his trauma buried beneath layers of addiction and paranoia. Through the lens of trauma-informed care, she saw beyond the surface behaviors and reached him in ways that others hadn't. "We found what worked—housing, routine, compassion. And his life changed."

That early success fueled Denise's advocacy for systemic change through AOT and trauma-sensitive approaches.

Cheryl: A Name, A Mission

Before she had her own center, Cheryl worked with individuals navigating psychosis, domestic violence, and substance abuse. But one woman—a survivor of intimate partner violence and chronic illness—taught her what transformation looked like. "She said therapy saved her life," Cheryl remembered. It was in the wake of this case that Cheryl birthed the idea for Metamorphosis Wellness Center. The journey of that one client helped inspire a place where many more could heal.

Chapter 28: Stories of Resilience and Healing

In the heart of clinical work lies a truth: healing is rarely linear, and resilience often emerges in the face of unimaginable adversity. These clinicians have walked alongside individuals and families navigating trauma, illness, and systemic neglect. Yet just as often, their own resilience was forged in the process. In this chapter, we witness not only the transformation of those they served—but the evolution of the clinicians themselves, whose compassion deepened, skills sharpened, and spirits endured through the very act of showing up.

Deirdra: Strength in Wholeness

As Deirdra's practice matured, so did her understanding of resilience. Working with individuals living with serious mental illness, she began to see beyond diagnoses and deficits. "It's not about fixing people," she says. "It's about helping them reclaim their wholeness." She recalls a client who, after years of hospitalization and system involvement, began setting personal goals again—starting with cooking a meal, then attending a support group. These small triumphs, Deirdra notes, are signs of deep resilience, sparked by the belief that life can get better.

Denise: From Systemic Failure to Systemic Change

Denise's work in public mental health and her leadership in implementing Assisted Outpatient Treatment (AOT) programs exemplify resilience at a systems level. But the most profound stories were personal. One client, discharged repeatedly from hospitals without coordinated care, came under her wing through AOT. Denise advocated across agencies, secured housing, and ensured consistent psychiatric follow-up. Over time, that client stabilized—and began mentoring others. "People can and do recover," Denise says. "But we have to believe in them first."

Guillermina: Rebuilding Family, Restoring Hope

Guillermina's career has been a series of lifelines cast to families on the brink. One mother, facing both addiction and the threat of losing her children, was initially resistant to help. Through months of counseling, home visits, and tireless advocacy, the mother entered treatment, regained custody, and found employment. "Her journey reminded me that support and belief can move mountains," Guillermina reflects. "Her children didn't just get their mom back—they got a future."

Sunita: From Silence to Self-Worth

A woman who once couldn't speak above a whisper began asserting her needs, attending social events, and exploring new relationships. For Sunita, that transformation embodied the essence of healing. "She learned to say, 'I matter,'" Sunita recalls. "That kind of growth isn't always visible to the outside world, but it changes everything." Sunita's own resilience deepened through grief—losing her brother, she says, allowed her to connect more authentically with clients navigating loss. "Pain taught me how to sit with theirs."

Scott: Breaking Through the Burnout

Scott's resilience emerged not only through the clients he served but in surviving toxic environments. Thirteen years in a high-stress setting supporting people with HIV and substance use nearly depleted him. But rather than walk away from the field, he transitioned to telehealth—rediscovering the joy of client connection in a new format. "I learned that healing isn't just for clients," he says. "We, as clinicians, need to keep healing too—sometimes by choosing a different path."

Paul: Reframing Stigma into Strength

Working in psychiatric admissions and leading support groups for individuals with HIV in the early '90s, Paul saw how stigma could crush the spirit. But he also witnessed extraordinary resilience. One client, recently released from prison and battling addiction, used group sessions to begin articulating dreams for the future. "He hadn't done that in decades," Paul says. "Hope isn't always loud. Sometimes it's just someone saying, 'I want more for myself.'"

Cheryl: Metamorphosis in Motion

Founding Metamorphosis Wellness Center was more than a career shift for Cheryl—it was a declaration of her belief in multidimensional healing. Through Reiki, meditation, color therapy, and traditional talk therapy, she has helped clients not just cope but transform. One woman, previously immobilized by anxiety, now leads yoga classes at the center. "People bloom when you give them light and room to grow," Cheryl reflects. Her center is not just a practice—it's a sanctuary of possibility.

Dara: Reimagining What's Possible

Through the REACH program and other initiatives for adolescents with developmental challenges, Dara has seen resilience manifest in small, powerful ways—like a nonverbal teen using art to express joy, or a young girl with autism attending a community dance. "When systems say 'no,'" Dara says, "we say 'how.'" These victories often came after months—or years—of persistence. "I've learned never to underestimate what's possible when someone feels seen and believed in."

Joy-Hee: Grace in Gratitude

After surviving the challenges of immigration and cultural adjustment, Joy-Hee built a career rooted in gratitude. Working with survivors of domestic violence and sexual assault in the Korean American community, she provided both advocacy and counseling—often the only person clients trusted. "Their courage inspired me," she says. "And reminded me why I do this work." The resilience she sees in others continues to reinforce her own.

Doug: The Gentle Revolution of Elder Care

Doug's work with older adults—particularly those in assisted living—has become a second act of purpose. "We tend to overlook the elderly," he says. "But they have stories, wisdom, and a desire for connection." In helping one older man rekindle a relationship with his estranged daughter, Doug witnessed a full-circle healing. "That moment didn't just change his life—it changed hers. And mine." His work reminds us that healing doesn't end with age—it evolves with it.

Chapter 29: Ethical Dilemmas and Integrity in Action

In the field of social work and mental health, practitioners are often faced with difficult choices that test their values, professional standards, and humanity. Whether navigating bureaucratic red tape, advocating for clients in the face of injustice, or confronting systemic failures, these clinicians chose integrity—again and again. Their stories reflect the moral courage it takes to uphold dignity, equity, and ethical practice in settings that don't always make it easy.

Deirdra: Leading with Values in a System of Compromise

While working with individuals experiencing homelessness and serious mental illness, Deirdra often found herself caught between institutional expectations and what she believed was right for her clients. In one instance, pressure mounted to discharge a client who had not "progressed" quickly enough. Deirdra refused. "She wasn't a data point. She was a person healing at her own pace," she recalls. Her insistence on individualized care not only safeguarded the client's wellbeing—it catalyzed broader conversations around ethical treatment timelines.

Denise: Advocating Across a Fragmented System

Coordinating care for individuals under Kendra's Law, Denise regularly encountered fractured systems that failed to communicate. When one of her clients with a history of violence was released from the hospital without housing or outpatient follow-up, Denise pushed back—escalating the matter to higher authorities until her client received appropriate services. "The easy path would've been to document and walk away," she admits. "But ethically, I couldn't accept a system failure as the client's failure." Her relentless advocacy became a model for coordinated, ethical care.

Guillermina: Holding the Line in Family Advocacy

Guillermina once supervised a case involving a mother accused of neglect due to substance use. Despite evidence of the mother's progress and bond with her child, external pressures urged removal. Guillermina reviewed every note, every progress report, and stood before ACS to make the case for family preservation. "It would've been easier to follow protocol," she says. "But easier isn't always ethical." The family remained intact, and Guillermina's decision preserved both their future and her own professional integrity.

Sunita: Staying True Amid Systemic Pressures

Early in her clinic work, Sunita was instructed to push medication adherence and rapid discharge timelines for clients with trauma histories. But one client—a young woman with PTSD—needed a slower, trust-building pace. Sunita pushed back, advocating for an extension of care and more collaborative treatment planning. "I wasn't just treating symptoms—I was helping someone feel safe," she says. Her stand not only benefited the client—it reminded the team of what ethical, trauma-informed care truly requires.

Scott: Refusing to Compromise in a Toxic Work Culture

While working at a nonprofit serving people with HIV and substance use disorders, Scott was asked to conceal details from a funder to preserve a contract. He refused. "I knew I was putting my job at risk," he says. "But our credibility, and our clients' dignity, meant more." Though the fallout was difficult, Scott's decision reaffirmed his purpose. "Integrity isn't always easy, but it's non-negotiable."

Paul: Standing Firm Amidst Medical and Ethical Tensions

At Stony Lodge Hospital, Paul once encountered a case where a young man's psychiatric commitment was being extended due to family pressure, despite his clinical stabilization. Paul advocated for the patient's right to autonomy, challenging attending psychiatrists and family alike. "It wasn't about defiance—it was about ethics," Paul explains. The patient was ultimately discharged, and Paul's advocacy prompted new internal discussions about patient rights and consent.

Cheryl: Creating Safe Spaces for Survivors—and Staff

In founding Metamorphosis Wellness Center, Cheryl faced dilemmas beyond therapy—such as how to protect the privacy of trauma survivors in group settings or how to address staff burnout without compromising client care. "Sometimes ethical choices aren't dramatic—they're in the quiet decisions," she says. From mandating regular supervision to instituting healing spaces for clinicians, Cheryl ensured that integrity shaped every layer of her center's culture.

Dara: The Ethics of Innovation in Care

When Dara proposed the REACH program for youth with pervasive developmental disorders, she was warned it might stretch resources and draw scrutiny. Still, she pressed forward—ethically unwilling to leave this population underserved. "We were treating kids who didn't 'fit' anywhere else," she recalls. "Doing nothing would've been the unethical choice." The program's success became a powerful example of how ethical imperatives can fuel innovation.

Joy-Hee: Cultural Competency as Ethical Mandate

While working with Korean American survivors of domestic violence, Joy-Hee often found that mainstream protocols—such as urging immediate shelter use—did not align with her clients' cultural contexts or safety needs. Instead of following rigid mandates, she took the time to listen and co-create safety plans. "Respecting culture is an ethical obligation," she says. "My job wasn't to 'rescue'—it was to empower."

Doug: Equity Over Promotion

Doug often found himself in meetings where lower-level staff were disregarded. Time and again, he redirected conversations to include their voices—whether they were aides, custodians, or assistants. When warned this approach could hurt his career, Doug didn't flinch. "I'm not here to climb ladders—I'm here to lift people up," he says. His quiet refusal to compromise on fairness became his most enduring legacy.

These stories remind us that ethical practice isn't reserved for rare moments of crisis. It lives in the day-to-day decisions—how we show up, who we listen to, and what we choose when the easy way out tempts us most. Integrity, in the lives of these clinicians, is not just a value—it's a way of being.

Chapter 30: Moments of Doubts and Breakthrough

Every clinician, no matter how seasoned, will at some point ask: "Am I doing the right thing? Am I enough for this work?" These moments of uncertainty, while often painful, hold within them the seeds of transformation. In this chapter, we witness how doubt gave way to insight, how personal and professional challenges became turning points, and how vulnerability, when embraced, led to clarity, confidence, and renewed purpose.

Deirdra: When Systems Seemed Too Broken to Fix

In the thick of bureaucracy, Deirdra once found herself questioning the very purpose of her role. She was overwhelmed by paperwork, systemic delays, and a lack of resources. "I felt like a cog in a machine," she admitted. But a breakthrough came when she chose to focus on one client at a time. Shifting her attention from institutional barriers to individual strengths reminded her why she started. That clarity reignited her passion and allowed her to influence the system from within, rather than be swallowed by it.

Denise: Learning to Let Go of the Outcome

Early in her work with trauma survivors, Denise often carried the burden of their recovery as her own. She doubted her abilities when clients relapsed or disengaged from treatment. It wasn't until a colleague reminded her, "We're not here to fix—we're here to witness and walk beside," that Denise experienced a shift. She began to trust the process more deeply and allow clients to lead. This moment of letting go became a turning point in her practice and her peace of mind.

Guillermina: From Exhaustion to Empowerment

While managing multiple roles across hospital units and school systems, Guillermina began to experience burnout. The constant juggling left her questioning if she could sustain her career. But a conversation with a former student she had supervised, who now thrived as a social worker, brought everything into focus. "She told me I was her model for perseverance and balance," Guillermina said. That affirmation reminded her that her presence was powerful, even when she couldn't do everything. She recommitted to self-care and mentorship, finding renewed energy through legacy.

Sunita: Learning to Protect Her Light

Sunita's empathy was once her greatest strength—and her Achilles' heel. Absorbing her clients' pain led her to emotional depletion, and she questioned whether she was cut out for the field. The breakthrough came through supervision, where she learned that boundaries were not walls, but bridges. "I began to see that I could be deeply present without losing myself," she reflected. That realization allowed her to stay in the work with more sustainability, compassion, and joy.

Scott: When the Career Path Vanishes

After being laid off from a job he loved, Scott found himself lost and uncertain. "I wondered if I was dispensable—if maybe I'd peaked," he recalled. But within 30 days, he was offered a new position at One Medical, where he found himself working with a population he never expected—tech professionals. The shift challenged and redefined his skills. "I learned I was more versatile than I thought," Scott said. "The doubt pushed me into a new chapter I didn't even know I needed."

Paul: Facing Himself in the Work

Moderating group sessions with people who had experienced incarceration and addiction, Paul sometimes felt unworthy. "I was young. I hadn't lived their lives. I thought, 'Who am I to guide them?'" he shared. But the breakthrough came when one client said, "You didn't come here to fix us. You came here to listen. And that's enough." That moment reframed Paul's role—not as the expert, but as the ally—and became the cornerstone of his clinical philosophy.

Cheryl: When the Vision Felt Too Big

Starting Metamorphosis Wellness Center was a leap of faith—and self-doubt followed close behind. Cheryl worried whether people would embrace a holistic model of therapy. "There were nights I thought I'd made a mistake," she said. But one day, a client who had been silent for months said, "This place gave me back to myself." That breakthrough erased her doubt. Her center, once a dream, had become a sanctuary.

Dara: Hearing "No" as Redirection

When funding for a girls' program she had developed was cut, Dara felt devastated. She had poured her heart into the initiative. But instead of giving up, she redirected her energy to building a campus specifically for youth with complex developmental needs. "The 'no' didn't mean failure," she said. "It meant I needed to build something even bigger." The loss became a launchpad for broader impact.

Joy-Hee: When Language Became the Bridge

Struggling with English during her social work training, Joy-Hee often felt invisible. "I doubted whether I could ever really connect," she admitted. But her clients—particularly within the Korean American community—saw her not as limited, but relatable. "You speak our language. You understand us," one client told her. That affirmation transformed her self-perception. What she thought was her weakness had become her superpower.

Doug: Redefining Success

Doug's dual identity as a lawyer and social worker made him feel like an outsider in both fields. He often questioned whether he had chosen the wrong path. But when he began working with older adults in assisted living, everything clicked. "This is where I'm meant to be," he said. "All of it—law, advocacy, empathy—it comes together here." The doubt gave way to a profound sense of alignment and peace.

These moments of doubt didn't mark the end of the road for these clinicians—they marked turning points. In the uncertainty, they discovered resilience. In the discomfort, they found new direction. And in the breakthrough, they reaffirmed their purpose.

Section III: Preferred Treatment Modality

The Craft, How They Practice the Art and Science of Social Work.

Chapter 31: Theoretical Orientation and Framework

Beneath every therapeutic exchange lies a guiding philosophy—a theoretical orientation that shapes not just interventions, but the very lens through which clinicians see their clients. For the clinicians in this chapter, theory is not static or dogmatic. It is a dynamic compass, pointing them toward meaning, connection, and transformation. Whether rooted in the deep inquiry of psychoanalysis, the directness of cognitive-behavioral therapy, or the sacredness of presence, these frameworks reveal a reverence for the complex, layered nature of the human experience.

Lorie: Psychoanalysis and Presence

Lorie's journey into psychoanalytic training was not merely academic—it was a personal pilgrimage into the recesses of the human psyche. This exploration equipped her with tools to navigate the unseen terrain of human behavior. But her theoretical foundation didn't end there. Alongside the analytic frame, Lorie discovered yoga—a path of integration that fused movement, breath, and soul. Through this union of theory and practice, she uncovered a framework where insight meets embodiment, and where transformation unfolds not just in the mind, but in the wholeness of one's being.

Jay: The Depths of Empathic Inquiry

Jay's clinical compass is rooted in psychoanalytic theory, but it is his profound empathy and authenticity that breathe life into his framework. For him, the analytic frame is not about interpretation alone—it's about presence, about sitting with someone in their truth and offering them the space to rewrite their story. His commitment to psychoanalytic depth is matched only by his ability to attune, to listen beneath the surface, and to make the invisible visible with compassion and care.

AnnMarie: Taoism, Meditation, and the Quiet Mind

AnnMarie's framework flows like a gentle river, guided by the teachings of mindfulness, meditation, and Taoism. Her studies in psychotherapy were not limited to technique; they were an invitation to embody a way of being—one that is peaceful, observant, and attuned to the rhythms of life. She doesn't just practice therapy; she lives it, embodying the serenity she hopes to cultivate in her clients.

Stuart: Carl Rogers and the Power of Not Knowing

Stuart found his theoretical north star in the teachings of Carl Rogers. He is guided by the belief that deep change requires deep listening—not knowing, but un-knowing—so that a client's own wisdom can surface. His respect for the therapeutic process, especially group therapy, stems from Rogers' radical trust in the client's potential. In Stuart's hands, theory becomes an invitation to presence, to empathy, and to the transformative power of relationship.

Cheryl: Gestalt, EMDR, and the Integration of Modalities

Cheryl's theoretical roots are both deep and wide. Grounded in Gestalt therapy and EMDR, she incorporates the teachings of the SWEET Institute to craft a holistic framework. She believes in the body's wisdom and the soul's capacity for healing, integrating traditional modalities with spiritual and somatic tools. Her approach is not about fixing—it's about lifting the veil of doubt so clients can remember their own power.

Paul: Person-Centered and Trauma-Informed

For Paul, theory is inseparable from trust. His person-centered, trauma-informed approach places the relationship at the heart of change. Whether supporting parents in crisis or moderating complex group dynamics, Paul's emphasis is on building safety, meeting people where they are, and honoring the dignity of their process. His framework reflects his belief that healing begins not with intervention, but with human connection.

Doug: Ethics, Empathy, and Listening as Theory

Doug's framework may not be found in a textbook, but it is no less rigorous. Grounded in an ethical, person-centered orientation, he integrates legal acumen with social work insight. His foundation is built on listening—on trusting what emerges from a space of presence and mutual respect. He believes theory should serve the person, not the other way around, and he remains guided by an unwavering belief in human dignity and the power of hope.

Chapter 32: Integrative and Eclectic Approaches

For many clinicians, no single theory or modality can fully capture the complexity of the human experience. Rather than adhere rigidly to one school of thought, these practitioners have chosen a more integrative path—combining techniques, philosophies, and personal wisdom into an adaptable, client-centered framework. Their work is a creative tapestry woven from years of experience, intuition, and a deep respect for the uniqueness of each person they serve.

Deirdra: Narrative and Strength-Based Fusion

Deirdra's approach is guided by stories—not just the ones her clients tell, but the ones society tells about them. Through narrative therapy, she helps clients reclaim authorship of their own lives, shifting from narratives of defeat to ones of resilience and agency. She integrates motivational interviewing and solution-focused strategies, but always returns to the central idea: people are not their problems—they are the protagonists of their own becoming.

Margaret: What Works, Works

Margaret describes her approach simply: "Whatever works best for that person." Her eclecticism is rooted in humility and client empowerment. She draws from multiple modalities—CBT, strengths-based, solution-focused—while remaining attuned to cultural context and personal identity. To Margaret, theory is only valuable if it aligns with the lived reality and needs of the person in front of her.

Jeanne: Psychodynamic Meets the Present Moment

Initially trained in psychodynamic therapy, Jeanne's work has evolved into an integrative blend that includes CBT and mindfulness techniques. She views her eclecticism as a strength—allowing her to meet clients with tools that match their current capacity. Her work affirms that theory should serve as scaffolding, not a cage, and that flexibility is key to therapeutic success.

Denise: Trauma-Informed and Evidence-Integrated

Denise has spent decades integrating trauma-informed care with evidence-based approaches like EMDR, CBT, and motivational interviewing. Her eclecticism is deliberate and disciplined, grounded in research and shaped by personal and professional wisdom. She doesn't just use techniques—she weaves them into a framework that respects the body, mind, and context of each individual.

Yokasta: Schema Therapy Meets Cultural Awareness

Yokasta merges schema therapy and CBT with a culturally grounded approach that honors the identities of her clients. Having worked extensively with immigrants and families navigating structural barriers, she customizes her methods to address intergenerational trauma and cultural resilience. Her eclecticism is not just clinical—it's communal, integrative, and deeply human.

Scott: From Supportive to Solution-Focused

Scott's approach has transformed over the years—from early experiences in supportive psychotherapy to his current blend of CBT, ACT, and solution-focused therapy. He adapts fluidly across settings, tailoring each session to the needs of a tech executive, a young adult in crisis, or a long-term trauma survivor. His integrative style is informed by lived practice and grounded in a deep respect for change at all levels.

Dara: Thematic Integration, Client-Driven Care

Dara's toolkit includes CBT, DBT, insight-oriented therapy, motivational interviewing, and mindfulness—but it's how she integrates them that makes her work distinct. She begins with presence and partnership, adapting her techniques to meet individuals, couples, and adolescents exactly where they are. Dara doesn't impose a framework; she co-constructs it with the people she serves.

Marisha: Meaningful Relationships and Modalities

Marisha views the therapeutic relationship as central to healing. Her integrative approach blends CBT, DBT, ACT, and trauma-focused methods into a cohesive, client-driven process. But beyond tools, she brings authenticity, compassion, and deep attunement—ensuring that every modality is used not as a fix, but as a way to reconnect clients with their values and vitality.

Doug: A Conversation Between Disciplines

Doug brings together the languages of law and social work, combining structural insight with emotional intelligence. His eclecticism is grounded in listening and in trust—trusting that the right approach will emerge from dialogue, collaboration, and attention to the unspoken. In his work with older adults and families, his integrative approach is as much about ethics as it is about empathy.

Chapter 33: Innovations in Practice

Innovation in social work often arises not from theory alone, but from the courage to experiment, to adapt, and to imagine new ways of helping others heal. These clinicians have brought fresh ideas into their practice—not for novelty's sake, but to fill real gaps in care, reach underserved populations, and address needs that traditional models sometimes overlook. Their stories highlight creativity in action, showing how social work can remain grounded while also evolving with the times.

Cheryl: A Holistic Model of Healing

Cheryl's Metamorphosis Wellness Center is more than a clinic—it is a vision brought to life. Combining traditional psychotherapy with Reiki, color therapy, and music, Cheryl redefines what mental health care can look like. Her approach acknowledges that healing is multidimensional and that the therapeutic space must honor the mind, body, and spirit. She sees herself as a facilitator, guiding clients toward their own inner resources with tools drawn from both science and spirituality.

Ann-Elizabeth: Advancing the Human-Animal Bond

Ann-Elizabeth has transformed a deeply personal passion into professional advocacy. As a co-founder of Social Workers Advancing Human-Animal Bond, she's helped carve out space for animal-assisted therapy and the recognition of pets as integral to family systems. What was once viewed as fringe has become a growing field, thanks to her relentless effort to shift policy and practice to reflect the emotional depth of human-animal relationships.

Shannon: Building SEL into the School Day

As Director of Social-Emotional Learning at Brooklyn Charter School, Shannon developed a full-scale curriculum rooted in the CASEL competencies. She didn't wait for permission—she created weekly lessons, built a mentoring program, and introduced nontraditional offerings like the Chill Snow-boarding Program to expand students' emotional literacy. Her work reimagines what school-based mental health support can be, emphasizing early, consistent, and community-wide engagement.

Deirdra: Narrative Therapy as Advocacy

For Deirdra, stories are not just therapeutic—they are revolutionary. Her innovation lies in reframing narrative therapy as a tool for systemic resistance. By helping clients reclaim authorship of their identities in the face of historical and structural oppression, she transforms therapy into an act of social justice. It's not just about healing the self—it's about restoring dignity.

Stuart: Group Work for Collective Change

Stuart's belief in the transformative power of group therapy runs deep. Drawing inspiration from Carl Rogers, he has championed support groups as spaces for shared healing. He applies this not only in clinical practice but also in grassroots activism—leading community gardening and composting groups that merge environmental justice with interpersonal healing. For Stuart, innovation often begins at the intersection of connection and purpose.

Jose: Creating Inclusive Clinics for Immigrant Communities

Jose's founding of Southern Dutchess Behavioral Health Services was itself a groundbreaking act. He intentionally built a clinic that reflected the cultural and linguistic diversity of his community, hiring clinicians from various ethnic backgrounds and designing services around inclusion and access. This wasn't just about cultural competence—it was about creating a model of care where no one feels like a stranger.

Scott: Bridging Tech and Therapy

When Scott transitioned into telehealth with a startup company, he brought with him a wealth of clinical expertise—and an openness to learning. He helped shape virtual therapy services for a tech-savvy population, applying CBT, ACT, and mindfulness in new formats. His adaptability and creativity in this digital landscape made therapeutic care more accessible and relevant to a new generation of clients.

Karen F.: From After-School Programs to Mindfulness Coaching

Karen's early work in Beacon Centers involved building support systems from the ground up. Today, she continues to innovate by integrating mindfulness, journaling, and meditation into her practice—especially with older adults navigating grief and transition. Her ability to adapt over the years, to blend systems-level thinking with personal connection, embodies the essence of innovation in care.

Chapter 34: Use of Evidence-Based Modalities

In a field as diverse and dynamic as social work, evidence-based modalities serve as both compass and anchor. They guide interventions, reinforce accountability, and provide a shared language across disciplines. Yet, for these clinicians, evidence-based practice is never mechanical—it's adaptive, thoughtful, and always attuned to the unique context of each individual. This chapter honors the balance between empirical rigor and human nuance.

Olivia: Mindfulness Meets the Evidence

Olivia's approach integrates Dialectical Behavior Therapy (DBT), Cognitive Behavioral Therapy (CBT), and Acceptance and Commitment Therapy (ACT), but she delivers them with a grace rooted in mindfulness and somatic awareness. Her deep respect for the body-mind connection allows her to ground these modalities in clients' lived experiences, turning abstract theory into transformative healing.

Jeanne: A Blend of Psychodynamic and CBT

Initially trained in psychodynamic therapy, Jeanne found herself expanding her repertoire in response to her clients' needs. She now blends psychodynamic insight with cognitive-behavioral interventions, particularly for clients who benefit from concrete tools and a present-focused approach. This dual lens allows Jeanne to hold space for both the past and the present, depth and direction.

Yokasta: CBT and Schema Therapy for Generational Healing

Working with both elderly individuals and immigrant families, Yokasta employs CBT and schema therapy to address longstanding patterns of thought and behavior. These modalities help clients reframe inherited narratives, challenge internalized stigma, and improve their relationships. Her application of evidence-based practices is both culturally sensitive and deeply restorative.

Dara: Tailoring the Toolbox

With training in CBT, DBT, motivational interviewing, and insight-oriented therapy, Dara tailors her interventions with precision and empathy. She doesn't see evidence-based modalities as scripts to follow, but as tools to be skillfully chosen and adapted. Whether working with adolescents or adults, her practice is built on a careful blend of science and presence.

Denise: Trauma-Informed and Outcome-Focused

For Denise, evidence-based modalities like EMDR and CBT are essential components of trauma-informed care. Her work in Assisted Outpatient Treatment (AOT) was grounded in data showing reductions in hospitalization and incarceration. Yet what truly sets her apart is her ability to translate this evidence into outcomes that matter—safety, dignity, and hope.

Paul: Building Trust Through Trauma-Informed Care

Paul's use of trauma-informed principles goes beyond the checklist. He incorporates evidence-based practices like CBT into a framework of empathy and patience, particularly when supporting families in crisis. His methods are research-driven, but his results are human: trust rebuilt, connections restored, and resistance softened by care.

Karen F: Bridging Evidence and Everyday Life

Karen has integrated evidence-based strategies like solution-focused therapy and CBT into her work with seniors and families. But she understands that the most effective intervention is one the client can relate to. By combining structured approaches with mindfulness practices and real-life tools like journaling, she ensures that therapeutic gains last beyond the session.

Devorah: Blending Structure and Insight

Devorah's integration of CBT, DBT, and behavioral therapy reflects a commitment to both structure and soul. Working with individuals facing addiction and eating disorders, she applies these modalities with a nuanced understanding of relapse, motivation, and identity. Her work underscores the potential of evidence-based practice to not only manage symptoms, but to reshape lives.

Chapter 35: Intuition, Wisdom, and the Role of Presence

Beyond frameworks and modalities, something less tangible—yet equally vital—shapes the craft of clinical social work. It is the presence of the clinician: the way they listen, the silence they hold, the gentle nudge of a question at just the right moment. This presence is built not only on experience but also on intuition, humility, and a deep trust in the therapeutic process. In this chapter, we meet clinicians who have learned to listen not just with their ears, but with their whole being.

Stuart: The Power of Not Knowing

For Stuart, presence is rooted in curiosity and humility. Influenced by Carl Rogers, he embraces the value of "not knowing"—of letting go of the expert role and allowing each client's story to unfold on its own terms. His deep commitment to group therapy reflects his belief in the wisdom of shared experience. "Being present," Stuart says, "is sometimes more healing than anything we can say."

Marsha: Faith as Foundation

Marsha's therapeutic presence is infused with her spiritual beliefs. She approaches each client as inherently worthy, deserving of dignity, compassion, and love. Her intuition is guided by faith, but expressed through listening, validation, and respect. Whether leading seminars or holding space in one-on-one sessions, her presence alone often fosters deep transformation.

Lynwana: Humor, Humanity, and Holding Space

Lynwana's strength lies in her authenticity. She isn't afraid to use humor, to share pieces of herself, or to meet resistance with compassion. Her therapeutic presence transcends traditional roles, creating a space where clients feel seen, heard, and accepted just as they are. Her wisdom is in knowing when to lean in, and when to simply be.

Ruth: Humor as Healing

Ruth's intuitive use of humor softens resistance and opens hearts. She doesn't direct her clients; she walks beside them, helping them learn how to care for themselves. Her years of experience have taught her that healing isn't always serious work. Sometimes, it begins with a shared laugh and the recognition that we're all human.

Doug: Trusting the Conversation

Doug blends legal precision with emotional sensitivity, but it's his presence that sets his work apart. He listens deeply, trusts his instincts, and lets solutions arise organically. "The best work often happens in the in-between," he says—between words, between roles, between what's said and what's understood. His presence is a steady anchor in uncertain times.

AnnMarie: Taoism and Therapeutic Stillness

AnnMarie draws inspiration from Taoism and mindfulness, embodying a calm and reflective presence. Her therapeutic work is grounded in the belief that healing often emerges from stillness, awareness, and acceptance. She doesn't rush the process; she invites it gently, allowing her clients to discover their truth at their own pace.

Dara: The Gift of Attunement

Dara's presence is shaped by humility and reverence. She honors the expertise each client brings about their own life and uses attunement to respond with precision. Her therapeutic wisdom lies in knowing when to offer tools and when to simply bear witness. "You have to earn your seat in someone's life," she says—and she does, every time.

Deirdra: Narrative as Sacred Space

For Deirdra, being present means honoring the sacredness of story. She holds space for clients to reclaim their narratives and offers deep validation of their lived experiences. Her presence is quiet but powerful, rooted in the understanding that sometimes, the most revolutionary act is simply to listen—without judgment, without interruption.

Conclusion of Section 3

This section reveals that the true craft of social work lies not in choosing one modality over another, but in knowing how, when, and why to use each approach. It is in listening deeply, adapting skillfully, and embodying the belief that each person holds the potential for change. These clinicians are not just providers of care—they are sculptors of possibility.

Through their methods, their innovations, and their presence, they show us that social work is an art, a science, and above all, a profound act of human connection.

Section IV: Being Part of a Community

Chapter 36: The SWEET Institute Experience

Connection that Transforms: Where Learning Meets Belonging

In the often solitary path of clinical work, finding a space that nurtures both professional development and personal transformation is rare. The SWEET Institute has become that space for many—a community where clinicians don't just learn, but awaken. For those who walk through its virtual doors, it offers more than continuing education; it offers a community, a mirror, and a sanctuary.

For Lorie, the SWEET Institute provided tools she had long sought in her quest to disentangle identity from mental health conditions. "Anxiety and depression often become fused with who we think we are," she explained. "But at SWEET, I was given frameworks and language to help clients rediscover themselves apart from their diagnoses." What began as a search for knowledge became a spiritual and clinical metamorphosis, as she embraced mindfulness, compassion, and insight into the human condition—starting with her own.

Jay, whose psychoanalytic grounding had given him a strong foundation in reflective practice, found at SWEET a space to integrate his insights into a broader dialogue. The Institute became not only a place to teach, but to grow. By engaging with a diverse group of clinicians across disciplines, he found new questions to explore and new ways to hold space for his clients. "It was refreshing to be in a place where everyone was learning from one another—not competing, but collaborating," he noted.

For AnnMarie, SWEET was a mirror that reflected her multifaceted identity as a clinician, artist, and educator. "It was one of the first places I felt I could show up fully—where the parts of me that love Taoism and meditation were not separate from the parts that practiced rigorous clinical work." Through

SWEET, she found a language that harmonized both her personal philosophy and professional life.

Monique joined the SWEET community during the pandemic—a time when the isolation of remote work threatened to erode the sense of connection so essential to clinical life. "When I joined in April 2020, it felt chaotic at first. We were all adjusting. But then a course on self-expression changed everything." That course catalyzed a wave of connection, turning silent video boxes into shared spaces of vulnerability and joy. "We started turning our cameras on, sharing stories, laughing, even crying. It changed how I showed up—not just on Zoom, but in life."

Lydia echoed this sentiment, describing her time at SWEET as "far more than an academic pursuit." To her, the Institute was a rite of passage—a place of metamorphosis. "It gave me more than theory or technique. It gave me my tribe." Through the SWEET Institute, she forged connections that anchored her practice in both purpose and community.

Yokasta, who had spent her career bridging communities through school-based work and mental health advocacy, found that SWEET offered something she hadn't realized she was missing—a family. "I've had colleagues before," she said, "but this was different. These were people who truly saw me, supported me, and challenged me to grow." Beyond clinical learning, she discovered nourishment—emotional, intellectual, and spiritual.

These stories, while unique, echo a shared theme: The SWEET Institute is not merely a place for professional development; it is a living ecosystem of connection, reflection, and reinvention. It fosters a sense of belonging that transcends geography, time zones, and even disciplines. Here, clinicians are not only shaped by the curriculum—they shape it together, in real time.

In this chapter of their journey, each clinician encountered SWEET as a gateway—a threshold between isolation and community, theory and embodiment, learning and transformation. And like all thresholds, it was not just about entering a new place; it was about becoming someone new in the process.

Chapter 37: Learning in Community

Knowledge as a Shared Journey

In the landscape of clinical care, where burnout often lurks and isolation can shadow even the most passionate professionals, learning in community serves as both a remedy and a catalyst. For these clinicians, learning wasn't a solitary act of accumulation—it was a shared, lived experience. The SWEET Institute became their hearth, their classroom, and their collective mind.

Monique vividly recalls how a simple shift in course format turned learning from passive observation into active engagement. "At first, we were all just there—muted, cameras off, attending but not present," she said. But something changed when SWEET introduced a course on self-expression. "Suddenly, we weren't just learning concepts. We were learning each other." That course opened the door to shared vulnerability, and from that space, a true community of learners emerged.

The evolution of learning didn't stop there. Monique noted how SWEET's adaptability—its shift from day-long lectures to digestible, dialogue-based formats—reflected not just innovation but care. "They listened. They responded. They created a space where we could bring our full selves, and that made all the difference." For her and many others, SWEET became proof that education can be both rigorous and relational.

Lydia described her SWEET experience as an "academic sanctuary." It wasn't just the depth of knowledge that drew her in, but the communal spirit in which that knowledge was exchanged. "I didn't feel like a student in a lecture," she said. "I felt like a collaborator in a movement." That movement wasn't theoretical—it was lived, felt, and embodied in the moments shared with fellow clinicians who, like her, were not just seeking answers but transformation.

Jay found the communal model of learning to be a return to something more ancient and authentic: dialogue. "It reminded me of what learning used to be—before PowerPoints and webinars. It was about sitting with others, wrestling with ideas, growing through conversation." Through SWEET, he rekindled a sense of wonder that had long been buried beneath layers of professional routine.

AnnMarie emphasized how the community embraced her multidimensional self. "I've studied a lot—psychotherapy, mindfulness, art, Taoism—but I'd never had a place where all of it could live together. At SWEET, it could. I could." The learning wasn't compartmentalized; it was integrative, holistic, and expansive.

In a world where professional development often feels like a checkbox, the clinicians of SWEET have discovered something radically different—a living curriculum that breathes, listens, and evolves with them. Here, learning is not just what you do; it's who you become, together.

This chapter affirms that when learning is communal, it is no longer a transfer of knowledge—it is a transformation of being. And in that transformation, clinicians don't just sharpen their tools; they reshape the very field they serve.

A Circle That Holds and Elevates

Social work is often described as a helping profession—but even the helpers need help. Mentorship and peer support are the invisible scaffolds that sustain the people who sustain others. At the SWEET Institute and beyond, this web of guidance, solidarity, and encouragement has shaped careers, transformed identities, and reminded clinicians that they are never alone.

For Jay, peer support was not a sidebar—it was the curriculum. In the SWEET community, he found colleagues who were also teachers, students who were also guides. Every interaction was infused with the quiet but profound understanding that growth does not happen in isolation. It is nurtured through dialogue, challenge, and affirmation. "Sometimes," he reflected, "it's not the formal training that changes you. It's the one comment after a class, the moment someone sees you and says, 'I've been there too.'"

Yokasta described her SWEET colleagues as her "extended clinical family." In moments when work felt heavy or overwhelming, it wasn't just the knowledge that carried her—it was the knowledge shared by people who understood the stakes. Her SWEET peers weren't just supportive—they were wise, candid, and willing to be vulnerable. "They made space for my questions, for my fears," she said. "That's what makes this more than education. It's healing."

Ann-Elizabeth, who has mentored countless students, sees peer support as an act of legacy. "Every time I guide someone, I'm not just helping them—I'm continuing the chain. Someone did that for me. Now I do it for others." Her belief in reciprocal mentorship reflects a profound truth: that support doesn't just go downward or upward. It moves in circles, weaving through generations and professional stages.

For Guillermina, mentorship has been a calling as much as a role. Over her decades in education and healthcare, she has supervised more than 80 Bachelor's and Master's level social work students. But for her, mentorship isn't about overseeing—it's about illuminating. "I show them how theory lives in practice, how empathy meets paperwork, how advocacy gets done even when it's hard." Her students learn not just clinical techniques but courage.

Scott, who once supervised social work interns in HIV/AIDS services, speaks to the sacredness of holding space for new clinicians. "When you supervise someone," he said, "you're not just shaping their skills. You're helping shape how they see the world, how they see themselves." The weight of that responsibility was never lost on him. Even in a toxic work environment, he remained a source of steadiness and inspiration for those who looked to him for guidance.

Mentorship and peer support are the invisible heartbeats of the social work community—quiet, rhythmic, sustaining. In spaces like SWEET, where connection is valued as much as content, these relationships flourish. They affirm what every social worker needs to hear at least once: You're not doing this alone. We're walking with you.

Chapter 38: Collective Advocacy

When One Voice Joins a Chorus

Social work begins with the individual—but its true power unfolds when individuals unite. Collective advocacy is where personal conviction meets public action. It's where the stories of those served are amplified by those called to serve. For the clinicians featured in this chapter, advocacy is not just a component of their profession—it is a living, breathing ethic that animates everything they do.

Ann-Elizabeth embodies this spirit. As a founding member and current chair of Social Workers Advancing the Human-Animal Bond, she helped forge a movement where none existed. "At first, the idea was met with hesitancy," she recalled. "But we didn't stop. We built a case, created partnerships, and showed the world that human-animal relationships belong in clinical practice and public policy." Today, what was once dismissed is now recognized, thanks to voices like hers that refused to remain quiet.

Vilma's advocacy is grounded in fierce love—especially for families. She has stood boldly in courtrooms and RoI rooms, insisting that mothers deserve a fighting chance. Her push for extended homemaking services and her battles against unnecessary separations are more than case victories—they are systemic interventions. "Children belong with their moms," she says. "And when the system forgets that, it's our job to remind it."

Cheryl, whose work spans both traditional therapy and holistic wellness, sees advocacy as expansive. Whether lobbying for HIV/AIDS education in the early 1990s or establishing her own healing center, she has consistently pushed boundaries—on what healing means, who gets access, and how care is defined. Her philosophy is simple yet radical: "We are not just practitioners. We are vision holders."

Emmanuel brings advocacy into the workplace, making equity not just a talking point but a daily practice. As a leader in city and state institutions, he made it his mission to ensure every voice—whether physician, janitor, or aide—was heard and respected. "I wasn't seeking a promotion," he once said. "I was seeking fairness." In team meetings, he spoke for those who couldn't, lifting concerns to leadership and creating pathways for professional development and dignity.

Paul, shaped by early work in the HIV epidemic, knows that advocacy is often born from urgency. "In those early days, people were dying, and there was so much stigma," he recalled. "We had to fight just to be heard." That fight became foundational to how he practices social work—meeting people where they are, honoring their truth, and never backing down from injustice.

These clinicians remind us that advocacy isn't always loud. Sometimes, it's in a well-placed question, a refusal to let a client be dismissed, or the persistent pushing of systems toward justice. Sometimes, it's starting a movement. Other times, it's staying rooted in one. In every form, advocacy is the heartbeat of social work, and when it's collective, its echo can change the world.

Chapter 39: Belonging, Healing, and Identity

Where We Are Seen, We Begin to Heal

Belonging is more than inclusion—it is being seen, valued, and understood. In the healing professions, it is both the soil and the sunlight. Clinicians often create belonging for others, but here we explore what happens when they find it for themselves. This chapter delves into how being part of a nurturing professional community reaffirms identity, supports healing, and reinforces the deep human need to connect.

For Lorie, the SWEET Institute became a space not just to learn but to rediscover the foundations of healing. In her words, "Mental health issues can become fused with identity. SWEET helped me develop the nuanced tools to help others separate from that fusion—to rediscover who they are without their diagnosis." Her evolution from treating symptoms to guiding people back to their wholeness reflects the Institute's deeper ethos: that healing begins with how we see each other.

Monique found belonging in the midst of global upheaval. When the pandemic forced professionals into isolation, SWEET became a lifeline. "At first, it was chaotic. But then, something shifted. We turned on our cameras. We started talking. We shared stories. And suddenly, we weren't just taking courses—we were building community." The Institute's evolution—into a space of mutual witnessing and affirmation—marked a turning point for her and many others.

Lydia describes her SWEET experience as a metamorphosis. "It wasn't just education—it was transformation," she said. Through connection with colleagues and mentors, Lydia not only grew professionally but stepped into a deeper version of herself. The feeling of being part of a 'tribe' gave her the courage to expand, risk, and trust again.

Yokasta shares this sentiment. Her voice softens as she speaks of her "SWEET family." For her, the community offers more than knowledge—it offers emotional refuge. "They understand me," she says simply. That understanding, that sense of being held and mirrored, is what enables her to do the same for others.

AnnMarie discovered that in a field often defined by burnout and fragmentation, SWEET offered integration. It affirmed her unique style and wide-ranging interests, giving her permission to be both clinical and creative, intellectual and intuitive. In doing so, it helped her align her professional identity with her authentic self.

In the mosaic of the SWEET community, each clinician's story became a tile—unique, essential, beautiful. Together, they crafted a vision of what healing looks like when it is grounded in mutual respect, shared purpose, and collective becoming.

Belonging doesn't just nourish—it transforms. It is the difference between surviving and thriving, between showing up and being seen. In finding community, these clinicians found themselves—and in doing so, became even more powerful agents of healing for others.

Concluding Reflection for Section 4

As this section draws to a close, what emerges is a tapestry of connection—woven not just through shared professional interests but through vulnerability, purpose, and trust. For these clinicians, community is not a passive backdrop but an active force in their growth and healing. It is a crucible where learning becomes wisdom, isolation gives way to collaboration, and identity is reaffirmed through belonging. Whether through the SWEET Institute or through grassroots efforts in their neighborhoods, they have found spaces where they are seen, heard, and valued. In turn, they have become spaces of refuge and renewal for others. In a world where burnout looms and silos persist, their stories remind us that community is not a luxury—it is the lifeblood of sustainable, transformative care.

Section V: Advice for Other Clinicians

Chapter 40: Avoiding Burnout and Compassion Fatigue

The Transmission – Wisdom Passed on from Experience

In the field of mental health and social work, burnout and compassion fatigue are not abstract threats—they are ever-present risks that can quietly erode the clarity, empathy, and sense of purpose that practitioners work so hard to maintain. Burnout, as first defined by psychologist Herbert Freudenberger (1974), is a state of physical and emotional exhaustion often accompanied by a sense of reduced accomplishment and depersonalization. Compassion fatigue, on the other hand, refers to the emotional residue or strain of exposure to working with those suffering from the consequences of traumatic events (Figley, 1995). Together, these phenomena can hinder not only the well-being of clinicians but also the quality of care provided to those they serve.

The clinicians featured in this chapter offer more than just warnings—they offer lived wisdom, strategies, and gentle reminders rooted in both experience and scholarship.

Alishka: Self-Care and Financial Realism

Alishka speaks candidly to those entering the field: "It's emotionally rewarding work, but let's be real—this work can also be financially and emotionally draining." Her advice to aspiring social workers includes being financially prepared and having a long-term vision. She encourages fellow clinicians to think about sustainable income models, including entrepreneurship, as a way to prevent burnout tied to chronic undercompensation. Her pragmatic lens aligns with the ecological systems theory (Bronfenbrenner, 1979), which emphasizes the need to consider how external systems—including financial structures—impact individual well-being and career sustainability.

Margaret: Purpose Over Personal Healing

In her role as mentor, Margaret offers a powerful call for self-reflection: "Be clear about why you're in this field. If you're here primarily to heal yourself, the work can become overwhelming." Her insight speaks to the importance of boundary awareness and the risks of enmeshment, concepts explored by theorists like Virginia Satir and Carl Jung. Margaret's voice serves as a reminder that while personal experience can be a powerful motivator, it must be integrated with self-awareness, supervision, and ongoing growth to avoid burnout and compassion fatigue.

Scott: Trusting the Process and Yourself

Scott offers succinct but resonant advice: "Trust the process. Trust yourself. Never stop learning." His words align with the concept of vicarious resilience—the positive transformation clinicians may undergo by witnessing client growth and healing (Hernandez et al., 2007). This perspective shifts the narrative from inevitable depletion to potential renewal, highlighting the capacity for clinicians to be inspired by the strength of those they serve.

Emmanuel: Service, Not Status

Emmanuel, who spent decades in public service, reflects: "You shouldn't be in this work for its material benefits. Do it out of love for humanity." His advice speaks to the humanistic theories of Carl Rogers and Abraham Maslow, reminding clinicians that fulfillment often stems from purpose and authentic connection rather than accolades or compensation. His words also caution against disillusionment, particularly when systemic challenges make the work feel thankless or invisible.

Lorie: Reimagining the Practice Space

Lorie's entry point to avoiding burnout was rediscovering learning and meaning. "The SWEET Institute came at a time when the world and my practice were in flux. It gave me something to hold onto." Her engagement with SWEET during the pandemic illustrates how belonging to an intellectual and emotional community can be a protective factor. Research by Maslach and Leiter (1997) emphasizes the importance of connection and community in preventing burnout—a theme Lorie embodies in both her story and her spirit.

Conclusion

What emerges from these accounts is not a one-size-fits-all solution but a mosaic of strategies and values. From setting boundaries and staying connected to community, to reevaluating motives and embracing financial realism, these clinicians offer a multifaceted framework for thriving in a high-stakes profession. As burnout continues to affect even the most passionate practitioners, these voices remind us that care must be reciprocal. To sustainably care for others, we must also learn to care for ourselves—with rigor, honesty, and compassion.

Chapter 41: Continuous Learning and Humility

In the ever-evolving landscape of mental health, the most effective clinicians are those who embrace a posture of curiosity and humility. As Paulo Freire (1970) notes in Pedagogy of the Oppressed, the most meaningful learning is dialogical—rooted in mutual exchange and continual reflection. For mental health professionals, humility is not a deficit but a discipline. It allows space for growth, for error, for questioning long-held assumptions, and for embracing what philosopher Donald Schön (1983) called the reflective practitioner—one who is never finished learning.

This chapter features clinicians who speak to the essential role that continuous learning plays—not just in refining technique, but in deepening humanity.

Jay: Speaking Their Language

Jay keeps it simple: "Speak their language. Walk with them." This orientation to learning isn't found in textbooks—it's found in the everyday practice of bearing witness. His approach, grounded in authenticity and deep listening, echoes Carl Rogers' client-centered theory, in which true presence and attunement are the most powerful tools a clinician possesses. Jay shows us that humility is often embodied, not declared, and that the willingness to listen is the first form of learning.

AnnMarie: Never Too Late to Start Again

AnnMarie offers an invitation, not just advice. Her story is a testament to lifelong learning—not as a luxury, but as a form of liberation. Her journey was not linear, but each step taught her something new about herself, her community, and the field. Her insight mirrors D.W. Winnicott's ideas around the "good enough" process—not perfection, but progression. She reminds us that professional growth is a series of becoming, rather than a destination.

Lorie: Learning as Sanctuary

During a time of professional uncertainty and global crisis, Lorie stumbled upon the SWEET Institute's offerings while searching for CEUs. What she found wasn't just knowledge— it was sanctuary. "It offered fresh perspectives when the world and my practice were in flux." This speaks to the importance of accessible, relevant, and transformative continuing education—something SWEET champions through experiential learning and integrative approaches. Lorie's story is a living reminder that we never outgrow the need for inspiration.

Someeka: Learning by Doing, Learning by Sharing

Someeka embodies the idea that we teach what we most need to learn. Her five-year journey with the SWEET Institute transformed her not only as a clinician but also as a person. "Their teaching style resonates with me, and I've applied many of their techniques with my clients." Her commitment to sharing resources and techniques reflects Albert Bandura's social learning theory: we learn by watching others, practicing together, and daring to integrate new approaches into our own unique voice.

Emmanuel: From Policy to Practice—and Back Again

Emmanuel's path bridges theory and action. His passion for policy work is not abstract—it's fueled by a desire to teach students that learning doesn't stop at licensure. "Policy work can be as powerful as clinical work, if not more so." His teaching aims to cultivate both competence and conscience, reminding us of bell hooks' vision of education as a practice of freedom—where learning is tied not just to knowledge but to justice.

Conclusion

Learning is not a phase; it is a rhythm. A rhythm of reflection, curiosity, trial, and connection. The clinicians in this chapter remind us that continuous learning is not just about clinical effectiveness—it's about remaining human, present, and awake. Whether through formal training, shared wisdom, or daily self-reflection, they show that the best therapists never stop learning—and never stop being transformed by what they learn.

Chapter 42: Advocacy and Self-Empowerment

In the practice of social work and mental health, advocacy is not an optional extra—it is intrinsic to the profession. Whether clinicians are speaking out on behalf of their clients, navigating complex systems, or asserting their own needs within institutional frameworks, advocacy and self-empowerment form a vital axis of effective care. This chapter highlights clinicians who see their own empowerment as a prerequisite for empowering others, demonstrating that the therapeutic alliance is not just interpersonal—it is also political.

As Audre Lorde reminds us, "Caring for myself is not self-indulgence, it is self-preservation, and that is an act of political warfare." These clinicians show us what it means to advocate for others while modeling the courage to advocate for themselves.

Monique: Joining a Movement, Not Just an Institute

For Monique, joining the SWEET Institute was more than continuing education—it was a declaration of alignment with a movement. "The SWEET Institute doesn't just stand as an institute—it symbolizes a collective stride toward a more compassionate, effective, and unified approach to care." Her sense of advocacy is inseparable from the collective, echoing feminist relational theory, which posits that empowerment and connection are mutually reinforcing. Monique's story calls clinicians to be part of communities that model what they hope to cultivate in their clients: voice, vision, and agency.

Daniel: From Member to Messenger

Daniel doesn't mince words: "I am a proud member of the SWEET Family and would highly encourage you to become a member." His voice carries the conviction of someone who has found alignment. In a world where clinicians are often asked to compartmentalize their personal growth and professional training, Daniel's advocacy is wholehearted. He embraces the idea that we change systems not only by critiquing them but by building and promoting alternatives.

Margaret: From Healing to Political Power

Margaret's message to aspiring social workers is clear: examine your motives, know your purpose, and recognize that healing is deeply political. "I really feel like I'm being drawn to the more political arena... to advocate for those who often have no voice." Her perspective aligns with Paulo Freire's idea of conscientização, or critical consciousness—the process of becoming aware of social, political, and economic contradictions and taking action against oppressive elements of reality. Advocacy, for Margaret, is both personal and systemic—a bridge between compassion and collective justice.

Alishka: Practical Tools for a Sustainable Career

Alishka offers pragmatic advice grounded in experience. She emphasizes financial preparedness, encourages clinicians to think entrepreneurially, and reminds them to prioritize emotional support. Her voice reflects a systems-aware empowerment model—where clinicians are not only healers but also stewards of their own sustainability. Her advice invites professionals to think critically about how to care for others without losing themselves in the process.

Scott: Trusting Yourself Is Advocacy

"Trust the process, trust yourself, and never stop learning," says Scott. Embedded in this advice is a quiet but powerful assertion: that trusting oneself in a field full of external expectations and regulations is an act of inner advocacy. Scott's story reminds us that advocacy does not always require a microphone. Sometimes, it begins with a whisper inside that says, "I deserve to be here."

Conclusion

Advocacy and self-empowerment are two sides of the same coin. In a field where burnout is common and systemic injustice is pervasive, these clinicians teach us that standing up for oneself is not selfish—it is necessary. And by doing so, they model a form of leadership that is both grounded and transformative. The empowered clinician is not the one who has all the answers, but the one who dares to speak, to question, and to create space—for themselves, and for others.

Chapter 43: Maintaining Boundaries and Integrity

In the field of mental health and social work, boundaries are often misunderstood as barriers—cold, rigid, impersonal. But seasoned clinicians know otherwise: boundaries are the invisible structures that preserve the safety, dignity, and integrity of both client and clinician. Without them, empathy becomes enmeshment, and advocacy becomes overreach.

This chapter delves into the lived wisdom of clinicians who have learned—often through difficulty—that maintaining boundaries is not just about saying "no"; it's about saying "yes" to a sustainable, ethical practice. Through their reflections, we glimpse what it means to practice relational integrity: a commitment to authenticity, accountability, and the long game of trust.

Jeanne: Leading with Compassion and Discernment

Jeanne's advice to aspiring mental health professionals is simple but profound: "Slow down before judging anyone. You never know what it's like to be in someone else's shoes. And remember, it's not always about you." Her words point to the nuanced art of holding empathy without assumption—a boundary of perspective. Her ability to recognize her own reactions and maintain therapeutic neutrality aligns with core tenets of psychodynamic theory: that awareness of the therapist's countertransference is essential to ethical and effective care.

Devorah: Holding Space, Not Holding Control

For Devorah, integrity means resisting the urge to "fix." She explains: "Create a space where clients can explore their own paths." This reflects Carl Rogers' client-centered framework, which emphasizes unconditional positive regard and the client's capacity for self-direction. In a world quick to prescribe solutions, Devorah's boundary-setting is a radical act: she trusts the client's wisdom and does not override it with her own agenda. Her boundary is trust itself.

Lorie: The Boundary Between Technique and Dogma

Lorie's critique of one-size-fits-all models is not just theoretical—it's ethical. She celebrates the SWEET Institute's commitment to pluralism, noting that "reducing suffering requires a spectrum of methodologies." Her insight reflects a boundary between integrity and indoctrination, reminding us that flexibility is not a lack of standards—it's a sign of maturity. Boundaries are not just about emotional containment; they also define the intellectual humility required for lifelong learning.

Emmanuel: Honoring the Hierarchy of Dignity

Emmanuel's stance on workplace hierarchy is deeply rooted in integrity. He ensured that voices—from physicians to housekeepers—were treated with equal respect. "I am the person in charge," he told his colleagues, "but my commitment to equity will not waiver." His words reflect the social justice tradition in social work, where boundary-setting includes resisting systemic disrespect. Integrity, in Emmanuel's case, meant holding power responsibly and modeling inclusivity at every level.

Conclusion

Boundaries are not the antithesis of connection—they are its precondition. These clinicians show us that boundaries, when grounded in clarity and care, become the scaffolding for trust, transformation, and longevity in practice. Integrity is not a fixed trait—it's a continuous choice. And through their choices, these professionals remind us that holding space is sacred work, and it begins by knowing where we end and others begin.

Chapter 44: Staying Curious and Client-Centered

In a field driven by protocols, documentation, and outcomes, it's easy to forget the simple, radical power of curiosity. Yet seasoned clinicians know: curiosity is the lifeblood of meaningful therapeutic work. It keeps our vision fresh, prevents us from reducing clients to diagnoses, and reminds us to ask, again and again, "Who is this person before me—and what matters to them?"

This chapter highlights clinicians who remain open to surprise, challenge, and the wisdom of their clients. Their work exemplifies the relational stance known in many therapeutic traditions as the "not-knowing position"—a posture that honors the client's voice as primary and recognizes that true expertise includes humility.

Jay: Speaking the Client's Language

Jay's philosophy is refreshingly simple: "Meet clients where they are, speak their language, and walk alongside them." This is more than rapport-building; it's a deep acknowledgment of the client as the expert in their own life. Rooted in humanistic theory, Jay's approach reflects a belief in the client's inherent capacity for growth and healing. His curiosity is practical—it informs a style of engagement that is direct, flexible, and deeply humane.

AnnMarie: Let Passion Lead the Way

AnnMarie's advice is less about specific techniques and more about attitude: stay open, stay inspired, stay human. Her narrative is a call for clinicians to live in alignment with their own passions and values. This alignment is not a luxury—it's a necessity. It fuels curiosity, renews empathy, and helps us avoid the emotional detachment that can come with burnout. In staying connected to her "why," AnnMarie models the client-centered ethic of authenticity.

Scott: Trusting the Process and the Person

Scott's guidance is both grounded and forward-thinking: "Trust the process, trust yourself, and never stop learning." His emphasis on lifelong learning reflects the reflective practitioner model popularized by Donald Schön, which views professional knowledge not as static but as dynamically shaped by real-world experience. Scott's trust in process mirrors the way he trusts clients—giving them space to grow at their own pace, without rush or rigidity.

Devorah: From Fixing to Facilitating

For Devorah, curiosity shows up in restraint. She resists the urge to offer solutions and instead focuses on creating the conditions for discovery. This mirrors the concept of "guided discovery" in cognitive therapies, where the clinician asks open-ended questions rather than providing direct answers. By allowing clients to make their own insights, she affirms their agency and preserves the collaborative nature of the work.

Jeanne: It's Not About You

Jeanne's reminder—"It's not always about you"—is an invitation to decenter the therapist. This humility is at the heart of a truly client-centered approach. It also protects against clinical arrogance, ensuring that clinicians remain learners, not just teachers. Jeanne models a relational ethic that is less about expertise and more about presence.

Conclusion

To stay curious is to stay alive—to stay awake to the unfolding story of each person we serve. The clinicians in this chapter show us that curiosity is not a naïve trait but a disciplined practice. It takes courage to let go of certainty, to listen more than speak, and to approach each session as an encounter with the unknown. But in doing so, we create the conditions where real healing can begin.

Concluding Reflection: Honoring the Transmission of Wisdom

In every profession, there are manuals, policies, and best practices. But in the healing professions, something more sacred is passed along: the transmission of wisdom. It is the subtle, lived knowledge that emerges from mistakes made and lessons earned—not just taught. It comes in the form of a question asked at the right time, a silence held with compassion, or a refusal to abandon hope when a client feels lost.

The voices in this section remind us that social work is not just a discipline; it is a lineage. Each clinician here has earned their insights through years of challenge, reflection, and connection. Their advice may differ in form—from practical reminders about self-care to philosophical reflections on presence and humility—but together they create a tapestry of guidance woven from the threads of lived experience.

They remind us:

- That burnout is not inevitable, but preventable through boundaries, meaning, and mutual care.
- That learning never ends, and humility is a sign of wisdom, not weakness.
- That advocacy must include the self—our needs, our values, our vision for what healing truly means.
- That boundaries are not walls but bridges to more ethical, sustainable practice.
- And that curiosity is not optional—it is the doorway to seeing the client, and ourselves, anew.

This section is not a list of tips—it is a torch being passed. A call to keep questioning, keep listening, and keep growing.

For in the end, it is not what we know, but how we show up—with openness, courage, and care—that defines the legacy we leave behind.

Section VI: What It Means to Them

The Integration: Personal Meaning and Professional Identity

Part 1

Chapter 45: Professional as Personal

For many clinicians, the professional is inseparable from the personal. Their work is not just a career—it is an extension of their identity, values, and purpose. In this chapter, we meet individuals whose clinical journeys reflect not only the development of skills and knowledge, but also deep personal transformation. For them, being a social worker or mental health professional is not what they do—it's who they are.

Lorie:

Lorie's work in mental health was already well-established when she found the SWEET Institute, but it was through SWEET's Socratic approach to teaching and the integration of Cognitive Behavioral Therapy (CBT) that her professional work and personal sense of mission fully converged. She describes the experience not as simply adding tools to her repertoire, but as opening a new dimension in how she thought about people, pain, and possibility. SWEET helped her to re-energize her clinical practice, not through more theory alone, but through application. In her words, the Institute allowed her to approach the complexity of mild to severe emotional conditions with greater clarity and confidence. The result was not just professional development—it was a deepened sense of alignment between who she is and how she serves.

Carrie:

For Carrie, discovering SWEET was not just a career move—it was a turning point in her life. What started as volunteer involvement led to a redefinition of her entire professional self. Through SWEET's coaching and courses, she was able to clarify not only what she wanted from her career but also why it mattered. The journey wasn't merely academic—it was soulful, introspective, and visionary. Her goals, once abstract, became grounded and tangible. What had previously been fragmented aspirations became a coherent calling. SWEET didn't just refine her clinical practice—it gave her a map to her future, one built on purpose and integrity.

AnnMarie:

AnnMarie's connection to SWEET felt like destiny. "From the moment of my birth in the Bronx, I was destined to unite with SWEET," she says. For her, the Institute became a spiritual and emotional home—a place where personal growth, professional passion, and a community of kindred spirits met in harmony. SWEET provided more than knowledge; it gave her a sense of belonging to something larger than herself. It reaffirmed her belief that the personal and professional are deeply intertwined and that healing work is as much about who we are as it is about what we know.

Daniel:

The pandemic became a catalyst for Daniel, leading him to SWEET in search of continuing education credits—but what he found was much more. Through immersive courses, check-in groups, and professional connections, he rediscovered his passion and deepened his sense of identity as a social worker. "It wasn't just an alternative to traditional learning," he says. "It was an elevation." He recalls printing out every course certificate with pride, not just as a record of knowledge gained, but as symbols of his commitment to his calling. The SWEET Institute gave him a professional language for what he had always felt internally: a profound duty to serve, grow, and heal.

Monique:

For Monique, SWEET's offerings started with professional interest, but quickly became deeply personal. Her early engagement was cautious and observational, but a course on self-expression became a gateway to personal transformation. Practices like mindfulness, journaling, and introspection helped her align her internal world with her external purpose. "The SWEET Institute," she reflects, "to me and many other professionals, is a transformative agent." Learning became a reflection of self-discovery. Clinical skills became mirrors for personal growth. The distinction between clinician and human being dissolved into a singular, integrated identity.

Lydia:

Lydia's relationship with SWEET began with a professional connection to its founders, but soon evolved into a meaningful journey of self-definition. Participating in SWEET's psychotherapy certificate course during a time of personal and global uncertainty helped her transition from apprehension to clarity. For her, SWEET became not just a place to learn—but a place to become. Through collaborative chats, innovative seminars, and human-centered teaching, Lydia experienced professional development as an unfolding of self. "It guided me," she says, "not just as a clinician, but as a person."

Ann-Elizabeth:

What started as a skeptical inquiry into CEUs soon turned into a profound shift for Ann-Elizabeth. SWEET offered more than credits—it offered a path to deeper meaning. She describes the Institute as a sanctuary in a transactional landscape, a place where clinicians become family, and professional development becomes a shared human experience. For Ann-Elizabeth, SWEET helped her remember that to be a social worker is not just a function—it is an act of embodiment. It is to live your values, advocate with courage, and foster healing by being wholly yourself.

Conclusion of Chapter 45:

Across these stories, we see a unifying thread: for these clinicians, professional identity is personal truth expressed through service. The SWEET Institute did not create their passion—it helped them remember it. It didn't give them a new identity—it reflected back to them the one they were always meant to embody. For them, to heal others is not a task—it is a way of life.

Chapter 46: Being a Healer, Advocate, and Witness

To be a clinician is not only to treat symptoms or apply interventions—it is to bear witness to the human experience. It is to step into stories filled with pain and possibility, to hold space for others while walking with them toward healing. In this chapter, we explore how these clinicians embody the role of healer, advocate, and witness, shaping their work through compassion, presence, and advocacy for justice.

Jay:

For Jay, the call to therapy is a call to deep human connection. He emphasizes authenticity, simplicity, and presence. "Meet clients where they are, speak their language, and walk alongside them," he says. Jay resists the trappings of clinical detachment and jargon, choosing instead to honor each individual's lived experience. Through SWEET, he found a space where his values were affirmed and his voice could echo in a community equally committed to healing. His work is not just about insight—it is about accompaniment, a sacred act of bearing witness with empathy.

AnnMarie:

AnnMarie views healing as a spiritual act—one infused with love, humility, and courage. Her work within the SWEET Institute is an extension of this belief. To her, being a part of SWEET means standing at the intersection of purpose and practice, where social work becomes not just service but sacred work. She credits SWEET with providing the community, inspiration, and tools to keep showing up for others with grace. As a healer and witness, she honors not just the stories of her clients, but also their strength.

Eugenia:

Throughout her career, Eugenia has lived at the cross-roads of advocacy and healing. A clinician, mentor, and leader, she has consistently extended herself to support others—not only clients, but peers and students. Within SWEET, she brings this same ethic of care. Her story reminds us that the role of witness extends beyond the therapeutic dyad; it includes how we stand for one another as professionals, how we model care in every relationship, and how we mentor the next generation to do the same.

DonnaSue:

DonnaSue's clinical work and her involvement in SWEET reflect her commitment to justice and healing, particularly within Black and Brown communities. For her, healing includes confronting the systems that perpetuate harm and stigma. She sees psychoeducation, cultural humility, and advocacy as therapeutic tools in their own right. Her work is a testament to how clinicians can use their voices not only to listen, but to speak—on behalf of those who have been silenced, and in the name of those who seek to be heard.

Monique:

Monique's clinical journey is deeply entwined with advocacy and bearing witness. She sees her role as both guide and student—someone who listens to her clients' truths while continuously learning from them. Her experience in the SWEET Institute strengthened her ability to stand at that threshold: to be a mirror and a companion, to teach and to learn. Monique reminds us that healing is not about fixing—it's about seeing, hearing, and believing people into their own strength.

Daniel:

Daniel's immersion into SWEET during the pandemic awakened a deeper understanding of his role as a clinician. Through courses, community dialogue, and collective reflection, he came to see himself not just as a therapist, but as a witness to transformation. His respect for the work is evident in the way he speaks about his clients and colleagues. To him, healing is a sacred collaboration, and SWEET offered a platform where this was not only understood—it was celebrated.

Olivia:

Olivia sees her therapeutic work as a deeply spiritual and embodied practice. With the SWEET Institute as her ally, she's deepened her ability to guide clients toward self-awareness, integration, and peace. Olivia doesn't just sit with suffering—she sits with the whole person. In doing so, she models what it means to be a healer: someone who doesn't hold all the answers, but who holds the space for someone to find their own.

Conclusion of Chapter 46:

These clinicians remind us that to be in this field is to be a witness to pain—and also to transformation. It is to hold space for complexity while offering hope. Through their connection with SWEET, they have found tools, language, and community to deepen their role as healers, advocates, and fellow travelers. In doing so, they elevate the entire profession and honor the sacredness of the work.

Chapter 47: Navigating Personal Values and the Work

Every clinician brings their whole self to the work—their up-bringing, culture, beliefs, and convictions. These personal values, consciously or unconsciously, shape every interaction, every interpretation, and every intervention. This chapter explores how members of the SWEET community consciously align their personal values with their professional roles, navigating tension, embracing authenticity, and transforming challenges into growth.

Ann-Elizabeth:

Ann-Elizabeth's path through the world of continuing education was marked by initial skepticism. Amid a sea of CEU providers focused on profit, she found SWEET—a space that resonated with her deeper values. Here, she was not just collecting credits but connecting with a mission aligned with integrity, service, and transformation. Her story reminds us that when our learning environments reflect our inner values, growth is inevitable and lasting.

Michelle:

For Michelle, maintaining alignment with her values has been central to navigating professional transitions. Whether responding to shifts in managed care or adapting to telehealth during the pandemic, her compass has been her unwavering commitment to personal and professional growth. With the SWEET Institute, she found not only advanced tools and concepts but also a community that honors curiosity, humility, and lifelong learning—the very principles that guide her clinical practice.

Carrie:

Carrie's journey with SWEET began with a spirit of service—volunteering for an event—but soon grew into something deeply meaningful. The Institute's coaching curriculum allowed her to explore her values, clarify her aspirations, and align her career with her true purpose. SWEET didn't just educate her—it helped her integrate. Her story affirms that when we bring our values to the forefront of our work, we don't just grow—we evolve.

Monique:

Monique's values are rooted in empathy, justice, and reflection. When she encountered the SWEET Institute, she saw those same values mirrored back. Through courses like Self-Expression, she explored how her identity, voice, and advocacy are inseparable from her clinical work. SWEET provided the framework to honor her own transformation while guiding others through theirs. Her experience reveals how therapeutic work becomes most powerful when rooted in a clinician's lived and evolving values.

Daniel:

Daniel's account of his transition into SWEET is marked by resonance—finding kindred spirits and values amid professional isolation. As the pandemic restructured the landscape of mental health care, SWEET became more than a resource—it became a grounding force. Daniel's values of service, lifelong learning, and mutual support were amplified by his participation in an organization that practices what it teaches.

AnnMarie:

For AnnMarie, SWEET offered a sacred homecoming. Her values of kindness, joy, and service found their mirror in a community committed to purposeful healing. In her own words, her involvement was not a coincidence—it was destiny. SWEET did not just reflect her values; it deepened them, gave them language, and provided tools to bring them into every session and every story she witnessed.

Jose:

Jose's steady involvement in SWEET courses and discussions stems from a profound belief in collective growth and self-awareness. His values are evident in his consistent support of colleagues and his dedication to inclusive and thoughtful care. In the Institute, he found a space where those values weren't just respected—they were essential.

Conclusion of Chapter 47:

In a world of shifting systems and external pressures, these clinicians remind us that integrity is not simply about doing the right thing—it's about staying connected to who we are and what we believe. The SWEET Institute has served as a space where clinicians can explore, refine, and embody their values with confidence. In doing so, they not only enrich their practice—they ensure it remains deeply human.

Chapter 48: The Role of Spirituality, Ethics, or Justice

For many clinicians, the work is not merely professional—it is sacred. Whether inspired by spirituality, driven by ethical principles, or fueled by a sense of justice, their commitment runs deeper than duty. It reflects a calling. In this chapter, we explore how SWEET members integrate their spiritual lives, ethical frameworks, and social justice commitments into the heart of their clinical identities.

Married in Ethics and Mission: Michelle

Michelle's journey as a clinician has always been intertwined with an ethical imperative—to bring healing where it is most needed. During the COVID-19 pandemic, her response was not only professional but spiritual: a determination to stay present, to continue growing, and to serve others from a place of grounded wisdom. Her engagement with SWEET's community, courses, and masterminds reflected an ethic of service that goes beyond survival—it is about showing up in love, even in crisis.

Sacred Spaces: AnnMarie

AnnMarie describes SWEET as a joyful, loving, and giving space—a reflection of the spiritual underpinnings that guide her work. Her gratitude for her parents, her children, and her SWEET mentors is more than acknowledgment—it's a devotional practice. Her belief in a world rooted in love, justice, and healing manifests in the way she practices social work, and in the way she receives and gives wisdom. For her, SWEET is more than an educational institute—it is a spiritual home.

Guided by Purpose: Monique

For Monique, the work is a covenant. From the moment she enrolled in SWEET's Self-Expression course, she saw therapy not just as a technical field, but as a spiritual pathway of self-discovery, transformation, and renewal. Her journey has been about alignment—bringing together her purpose, her community, and her practices into one seamless flow of integrity. It is a spiritual integration that elevates her impact and sustains her through complexity.

The Justice Lens: Emmanuel

While not directly quoted in this section, Emmanuel's story runs throughout the SWEET community as one rooted in justice. His advocacy for equity, his refusal to let hierarchy silence the voices of nurses and housekeepers, and his commitment to mentorship are the embodiment of ethical social work. His values are lived, not stated—and SWEET offered a space that honored, encouraged, and expanded that mission.

Faith in Action: DonnaSue

For DonnaSue, her advocacy for mental health awareness in Black and Brown communities is a deeply ethical and spiritual act. Her commitment to psychoeducation, cultural humility, and stigma reduction is not merely part of her job—it is a ministry. At SWEET, she found a platform where this sacred calling could flourish—a place where social work is practiced with reverence and radical love.

The Soul of Community: Lydia

Lydia speaks of SWEET not just as a professional network but as a soulful community. In her reflections on the evolution of the Psychotherapy Certificate Course and the transformation it sparked in herself and others, she identifies something beyond knowledge—a shift in worldview. For Lydia, engaging with SWEET is an act of hope, a moral and spiritual investment in the future of the profession.

Conclusion of Chapter 48:

In a field often focused on outcomes and interventions, these clinicians remind us that at its core, social work is a sacred practice. Whether through prayer, justice, or compassion, their work is a reflection of inner convictions made manifest. SWEET has provided not only tools and knowledge but a container—where the sacredness of this work is honored, nourished, and passed on.

Chapter 49: Purpose and Meaning Over Time

With time comes clarity. For many clinicians, purpose is not found in a single moment—it evolves. Shaped by life experiences, personal transformations, and professional encounters, the meaning behind the work becomes more nuanced, more grounded, and more powerful. This chapter explores how clinicians' understanding of their purpose has deepened over time and how SWEET has helped illuminate that journey.

Carrie: From Aspiration to Aligned Purpose

For Carrie, SWEET was a place of integration. What began as volunteering quickly became a transformative experience. Through its coaching curriculum, Carrie found more than skills—she discovered a blueprint for purpose. What once felt like scattered aspirations became clarified goals. SWEET didn't simply provide direction; it reawakened her professional calling and gave her the confidence to pursue it with precision and heart.

Daniel: Reigniting the Flame

For Daniel, SWEET arrived at a time when the world was standing still. The pandemic disrupted his usual rhythms, but in the stillness, SWEET offered something vital—a renewed sense of mission. With every certificate course, every supportive check-in, he rediscovered not only what he knew but why he had chosen this path. His pride in printing completion certificates wasn't about credentials—it was about meaning restored, purpose rekindled, and a new chapter written with intention.

Ann-Elizabeth: From Compliance to Communion

Ann-Elizabeth initially approached continuing education as a requirement—but SWEET transformed it into a sacred opportunity. What began as a search for CEUs became a community of practice, a place where knowledge was humanized and meaning emerged from connection. Her sense of purpose expanded as she witnessed the collective energy of SWEET—a network that cared, that inspired, and that reminded her why she began this journey in the first place.

Michelle: Purpose through Perseverance

Michelle's story is one of resilience, determination, and clarity. Each challenge—managed care, the pandemic, the pivot to virtual care—deepened her commitment. Through her involvement in SWEET focus groups and accountability partnerships, she was reminded that meaning is not a destination but a practice. Her purpose is not something she holds—it's something she lives, in each conversation, each collaboration, and each courageous choice.

Lorie: Bridging Theory and Purpose

Lorie brought decades of wisdom to SWEET, but what she found was not just theory—it was transformation. The Institute's focus on Socratic teaching and actionable insights allowed her to bridge knowledge and meaning. Her purpose became clearer: to empower others not just through analysis, but through practical healing. SWEET helped make that mission more alive and tangible.

Monique: A Journey of Alignment

Monique's relationship with SWEET began with a search for skills, but it blossomed into something far deeper. Each course, each gathering, helped her refine her inner compass. She moved from being a participant to a co-creator, from learner to leader. SWEET allowed her to integrate her diverse roles into a coherent purpose—one rooted in authenticity, courage, and community.

Conclusion of Chapter 49

Purpose, for these clinicians, is not static. It's a living, breathing force—evolving with time, experience, and reflection. At every twist in the journey, SWEET served not only as a guidepost but as a companion. In helping them connect the dots between past, present, and future, SWEET has supported not just their work—but their becoming.

Concluding Reflection – Section VI, Part 1: The Integration – Personal Meaning and Professional Identity

By the time they arrive at this point in their journey, these clinicians are no longer simply practitioners—they are integrated beings whose personal histories, professional paths, and community engagements form a unified whole. The SWEET Institute has not merely provided continuing education or clinical tools; it has offered a space for transformation—where knowledge becomes wisdom, where technique becomes art, and where identity becomes purpose.

Across these five chapters, we witness how theory is made personal, how healing becomes reciprocal, and how values find their home in action. SWEET has served as a crucible—a place where people unlearn, relearn, and return to themselves more fully. In doing so, it has offered each clinician not just professional development, but a deeply human sense of belonging and meaning.

Their stories remind us: The work we do is never separate from who we are. And when a community holds us as we grow, we begin to live our work not just with competence—but with clarity, love, and purpose.

Section VI
Part 2

Chapter 50: Professional as Personal

For many of the clinicians whose voices form the living heart of the SWEET Institute community, the boundary between personal and professional is not a dividing line, but a point of integration. Their stories reveal how being a clinician is not simply a role they perform—it is who they are, shaped by life experiences, personal challenges, and the call to serve. The SWEET Institute, for them, has not merely offered training or knowledge; it has provided a mirror, a compass, and a community that helps them make sense of their lives as they help others do the same.

Marsha calls SWEET her "home away from home," a phrase that speaks volumes about the depth of her integration between her professional work and her personal growth. For her, the Institute is not just a place for professional development—it is a nurturing space that has profoundly shaped her identity. The education she receives is not isolated from who she is—it fosters self-discovery. "SWEET has shaped me into the person I am today," she says, underscoring the inseparability of her role as a clinician from her unfolding personal journey.

Lisa Marie shares a similar story. What began as a search for continuing education credits turned into a discovery of purpose and belonging. "What sets SWEET apart is the community," she explains. "Even something as simple as the WhatsApp group has created a space where I feel supported and connected." For Lisa, SWEET is not just about compliance with professional standards—it is about finding herself in the process, feeling seen, heard, and transformed by a community that aligns with her values.

For Doug, SWEET was an unexpected homecoming. A professional who straddles both legal and social work spheres, Doug found in the Institute not only advanced knowledge but a community where his hybrid identity was affirmed. SWEET wasn't just another platform; it was a space that gave meaning to his interdisciplinary work and a renewed sense of belonging. "Through its programs, I've refined my approach and built relationships with individuals who share my passion for making a difference."

Agnes, a clinician with decades of experience, echoes the sentiment. Despite her long tenure in the field, she found rejuvenation and fresh perspective through SWEET. The Institute offered her not only new skills but also a rekindled sense of personal mission—one that integrates compassion, care, and growth. "The Institute has enriched my professional journey and helped me stay grounded and connected," she says. In doing so, it has helped her reconnect to the foundational reasons she became a clinician in the first place.

Marisha, who lives in Cape Cod where professional networks are sparse, found in SWEET not just education, but a sanctuary. It became her lifeline, her intellectual and emotional wellspring, and a place where she could evolve not only as a clinician but as a person. SWEET's emphasis on presence, mindfulness, and self-awareness resonated deeply. "For me, it's a place where I continue to evolve," she reflects, capturing the Institute's role in shaping her professional being and personal becoming.

For Jeanne, the connection is equally profound. Her therapeutic stance, deeply rooted in listening, empathy, and non-judgment, mirrors the SWEET Institute's principles. "The Institute reminds us to see others fully," she says. SWEET validates the central philosophy that undergirds her practice: that clinicians and clients alike grow when they are met with presence, compassion, and curiosity.

Whether in New York, North Carolina, or Cape Cod, SWEET has become a place where professional evolution is deeply personal. For these clinicians, the Institute is not a distant institution; it is a reflection of who they are and who they strive to become. It is where their professional lives find meaning and where their personal truths are affirmed.

Chapter 51: Being a Healer, Advocate, and Witness

To be a clinician is to bear witness. To hold the stories that others carry, to sit with suffering, to see beyond the symptoms, and to stand beside someone as they reimagine their life. Within the SWEET Institute, many clinicians have found not only tools to heal, but the strength to advocate, the language to empower, and the courage to witness—with presence, humility, and grace.

Jeanne Weiner embodies this role through every fiber of her practice. Her integration of SWEET's strength-based, person-centered approach affirms what she has always known: that the most powerful change happens when we listen—truly listen. For Jeanne, SWEET doesn't just train clinicians; it teaches them to meet others with compassion and to help them discover their own capacity. This echoes her own belief that healing begins when someone feels seen.

For Sarah, the therapeutic process is also one of advocacy. Her belief in trauma-informed care and social-emotional learning is not simply theoretical—it's embodied. She views her work not just as a clinician but as someone actively reclaiming space for the voices of marginalized communities. Through SWEET, she has found a professional community that affirms this integration—where advocacy and healing are two sides of the same coin.

Stuart Aaronson, a longtime advocate and healer, resonates deeply with SWEET's mission of integrating consciousness into clinical practice. From group counseling to youth advocacy and now into creative, mindfulness-based therapeutic techniques, Stuart has always seen the clinician's role as one of soulful accompaniment. SWEET has become a space where his lifelong values—of listening deeply, of holding space, of elevating others—are not only welcomed but expanded.

Sol Reyes Pelosi, whose decades of work span foster care, family systems, and educational advocacy, finds in SWEET an ally to her life's mission. The Institute's commitment to understanding systemic issues and empowering families mirrors Sol's own approach: therapy is not just about individuals—it's about transforming the environments they live in. In SWEET, she has found the language, tools, and community to deepen this work.

Devorah, too, exemplifies the integration of healing and advocacy. Through SWEET, she has continued to refine a practice that resists the urge to "fix," and instead embraces the role of witness—one who supports clients as they uncover their own solutions. Her work, inspired by lived experience, reminds us that bearing witness is not passive; it is the active stance of trust, respect, and humility.

Denise, long committed to trauma-informed care, sees SWEET as a natural extension of her life's work. Whether she's coordinating public mental health services or advocating for survivors, Denise has always operated from a place of integrity and advocacy. SWEET's model aligns with her belief that clinicians are agents of systemic healing, working not just within therapy rooms, but across communities and institutions.

In these voices, we hear a shared understanding: clinicians are not just practitioners of a method. They are witnesses to transformation, advocates for justice, and healers walking alongside others in the sacred space of change. SWEET honors this by creating a platform where these identities are nurtured, deepened, and elevated.

Chapter 52: Navigating Personal Values and the Work

The journey of a clinician is not only about what we do—but about how we reconcile who we are with what the work demands of us. This chapter explores how SWEET Institute members navigate personal values, life philosophies, and moments of inner questioning while staying anchored in purpose.

For Lisa Marie, the alignment of her values with her clinical work was not immediate—it was discovered. Her introduction to SWEET came during a search for continuing education but became something far more personal. "What I discovered was a platform unlike any other," she shares. Beyond the trainings, Lisa found a community of kindness, integrity, and humanity. "Even something as simple as the WhatsApp group created a space where I feel supported and connected." In SWEET, she found a place where the professional and personal could co-exist—where empathy and ethics could live side by side.

Doug also exemplifies this integration. Coming from the world of law, he carried a unique dual identity into the field of social work. SWEET became a space where he could embrace both: the legal advocate and the empathetic clinician. In its community, Doug found a shared language of justice, transparency, and care. He describes SWEET as a place where "learning, exchange, and personal values aren't in conflict—they are welcomed as a whole."

Jeanne brings a deeply personal ethic to her work. Through her SWEET journey, she has leaned further into her understanding that healing requires empathy, humility, and non-judgment. Her values are inseparable from her work, and SWEET has been an affirming mirror—showing her that to be a clinician is also to be human.

Cheryl, rooted in a vision of transformation, found in SWEET not only advanced training but a space that aligned with her deepest convictions. "These methods align perfectly with my belief in the human capacity for self-healing," she explains. SWEET's strength-based, client-centered framework affirms her vision of therapy as a collaborative and spiritually grounded act—one in which clients are not "treated" but gently supported as they rediscover their wholeness.

Agnes, whose decades of experience include advocacy for families affected by domestic violence and trauma, appreciates SWEET's ethical depth. "It aligns with my values of care and compassion," she says, highlighting the institute's capacity to foster healing while holding space for complexity. SWEET, for her, represents not only tools and strategies but a living philosophy of how to serve with heart.

Guillermina, shaped by a legacy of helping instilled by her mother, finds SWEET's mission to be an extension of her own life's purpose. The Institute's emphasis on collaborative growth and equity echoes her own belief: that helping others is not just professional—it is personal. SWEET does not separate theory from humanity, and for Guillermina, that is exactly what allows the work to remain sustainable and meaningful.

For these clinicians, SWEET is not simply a place to earn credits or learn new tools. It is a space where values are lived. Where the ethical questions—of how to serve, how to heal, how to care—are not seen as distractions, but as the very soul of the work.

Chapter 53: The Role of Spirituality, Ethics, or Justice

For many clinicians, the work of healing cannot be separated from deeper questions of meaning, morality, and justice. Whether shaped by spiritual roots, ethical commitments, or a fierce drive for equity, these clinicians reveal how the SWEET Institute has provided both a sanctuary and a platform for exploring and embodying their highest ideals.

Marsha sees her work as inseparable from her faith. She describes SWEET not just as a community of professionals, but as a home away from home—a place where her spiritual values of service, growth, and compassion find expression in tangible ways. Through SWEET, Marsha says she has not only developed her skills but also deepened her understanding of what it means to live and lead with integrity. Her appreciation for the nurturing environment, she notes, reflects her gratitude for how SWEET has shaped her personally as much as professionally.

Denise, whose work has long centered on trauma-informed care and advocacy for the most marginalized, sees SWEET as aligned with a broader vision of justice. The Institute's systemic lens and person-centered approach resonate deeply with her lifelong commitment to ensuring no one falls through the cracks. For Denise, justice isn't just about policy—it's about presence. It's about showing up for people in their most vulnerable moments and helping to build systems where healing is possible.

Stuart, too, views SWEET as a place where ethics and transformation go hand in hand. From his early work in advocacy and youth programming to his current emphasis on integrating mindfulness, creativity, and community healing, Stuart sees SWEET as a spiritual and ethical extension of his life's mission. The Institute's emphasis on "not knowing," on truly listening, and on the dignity of every human experience mirrors the same principles he's held close throughout his career.

Paul, a quiet champion of dignity and inclusion, credits SWEET with helping him refine his trauma-informed lens. He values the Institute's capacity to equip professionals not only with technical skills but with the ethical awareness to "meet people where they are." For Paul, ethics begins with humility—and SWEET, in his words, offers "an education in humanity."

Sol, reflecting on her work with families and children, sees SWEET's commitment to systemic awareness and justice as essential. The Institute's integration of innovative clinical practices with a deep understanding of structural challenges mirrors her belief that true healing must account for the contexts people live in. Her time with SWEET has not only enhanced her skills but expanded her vision of what ethical, justice-oriented social work can look like.

In Sarah's work integrating trauma-informed care with social-emotional learning, SWEET's emphasis on healing the whole person—within the reality of their community, culture, and history—has provided both inspiration and validation. The Institute, she says, "embodies what's possible when compassion and justice walk hand in hand."

These clinicians remind us that ethics is not merely a professional code, and spirituality is not confined to a religious framework. Both are living commitments—practiced through presence, expressed in advocacy, and nurtured in community. Through SWEET, these values are not only honored—they are put into action, woven into the very structure of care.

Chapter 54: Purpose and Meaning Over Time

Time has a way of clarifying what truly matters. For these clinicians, the passage of years has not dulled their passion—it has refined it. Through growth, setbacks, reinvention, and recommitment, their sense of purpose has deepened. The SWEET Institute has become not just a companion in that journey, but a catalyst for renewed meaning.

Jenna, who first partnered with SWEET through her leadership at Goodwill, continues to hold the Institute as a trusted collaborator in her professional evolution. What began as a need for effective training blossomed into a lasting relationship that supports her commitment to excellence in care. For Jenna, SWEET represents the enduring power of aligned values—where education meets purpose and where clinicians are empowered to serve with clarity and conviction.

Steven, known for integrating CBT and psychoanalysis in innovative ways, speaks of SWEET as a touchstone that keeps him rooted in both tradition and growth. "It resonates with my style," he shares. "It keeps me up to date, challenged, and connected." As his career evolves, so too does his toolkit—and SWEET, with its blend of traditional and cutting-edge practices, offers a wellspring of continuing relevance and inspiration.

Yokasta sees learning not as a stage of life, but as a way of life. Her longstanding relationship with SWEET is a testament to that belief. With every course and connection, she finds new energy to face the complexities of school-based social work, cultural advocacy, and family healing. Over time, SWEET has become her mirror and her map—reflecting her growth while guiding her next steps.

Karen S., a seasoned clinician and leader, came to SWEET through curiosity—and stayed for the depth. Even after decades in the field, she finds the Institute refreshing, offering practical tools and rich insights that reinvigorate her clinical work. "It keeps my skills current," she says, "and brings me joy." For Karen, SWEET reaffirms that growth doesn't stop—it simply takes new forms.

Imee, reflecting on her diverse career across schools, clinics, and youth programming, calls SWEET a "significant milestone." It arrived at just the right time, offering supervision, training, and a deepened sense of alignment between her values and her work. SWEET, she says, gave her the confidence to serve more fully and to lead with authenticity.

Doug discovered SWEET while seeking legal education, but what he found was far more transformative. Over time, he realized the Institute wasn't just a source of information—it was a professional home. A place where his dual passions for justice and healing could coexist, evolve, and flourish. Today, Doug sees SWEET as essential to his ongoing journey—a space where his commitment to service is continuously renewed.

Marisha, living in Cape Cod, describes SWEET as a lifeline. In a community where professional resources are sparse, SWEET has filled the gap—providing not just knowledge but kinship. "It's where I continue to evolve," she reflects. For her, SWEET is a sustaining force, one that ensures her purpose remains vibrant, adaptive, and deeply rooted in compassion.

For all of them, SWEET is not a destination but a companion—walking beside them through the seasons of their work, reminding them why they began and supporting who they are becoming. In their stories, we see how meaning deepens not just through what we do, but through the community that holds us as we do it.

Concluding Reflection – Section VI: The Integration

By the time we arrive at this section of the journey, we are no longer only talking about careers—we are speaking of callings. The clinicians you've met here do not merely practice social work; they live it, breathe it, and embody its spirit in everything they do. Their work is not a task, but a testimony to resilience, compassion, and transformation.

The SWEET Institute has become, for many of them, the sacred meeting ground between knowledge and wisdom, between action and reflection, between the personal and the professional. Here, they have found not just strategies or interventions, but a framework for meaning—one that honors the human being behind the professional title.

Through their voices, we witness the merging of practice and purpose, theory and truth, solitude and community. We see how the work of healing others becomes a mirror for healing the self. And we are reminded that the greatest impact often arises not from expertise alone, but from presence, humility, and shared humanity.

In these stories, purpose is not a fixed point—it is a living, evolving force. It changes shape as the seasons of life shift, but it never fades. Instead, it deepens. And as it deepens, it guides.

Let this section stand as a tribute to that depth—to the clinicians who walk this path with courage, and to the communities, like SWEET, that walk alongside them.

Section VII: Where They Think Social Work Is

The Vision-Future Hopes, and Systemic Change.

Chapter 55: Innovations and Opportunities

The future of social work is not something we are waiting for—it is something we are actively shaping. Across disciplines and domains, clinicians are embracing innovations that once seemed out of reach. Whether it's integrating somatic therapies with trauma-informed care, applying neuroscience to behavior change, or reimagining the power of digital platforms, the social work profession is rapidly evolving into one of the most dynamic and interdisciplinary fields of the 21st century.

Lorie speaks to this transformation with hope and clarity. Her work with the SWEET Institute opened her eyes to new pedagogical and clinical tools—especially those grounded in cognitive behavioral therapy, motivational interviewing, and holistic integration. "Institutions like SWEET are leading the charge," she says. "They remind us that learning is a lifelong process, and they equip us with diverse tools to meet people where they are." This notion aligns with adult learning theory (Knowles, 1984), which posits that meaningful education must connect with real-world relevance and self-directed growth. The innovations in continuing education—like experiential learning, role play, and scenario-based inquiry—are helping clinicians bridge theory and practice in powerful ways.

Olivia offers a vision that combines equity and empathy. "I see a world where social workers are not just valued," she says, "but supported and empowered." For her, innovation is not merely technological—it is human-centered. "Healing," she insists, "must be accessible to all." This echoes the tenets of intersectional practice, reminding us that innovations must address systemic barriers and historical inequities. Olivia's work, which integrates mindfulness and body-based awareness with talk therapy, highlights how expanding the therapeutic toolkit allows for more inclusive and responsive care.

Jenna, too, looks ahead with passion. Her work in trauma-informed systems change is at the forefront of what the field can become. "Innovative projects aren't just about new techniques," she reflects. "They're about changing the way we think about care, power, and possibility." Jenna's commitment to institutional transformation—especially around trauma-informed supervision, policy advocacy, and team wellness—embodies the systemic perspective long called for by theorists like Bronfenbrenner (1979) and organizations like the National Child Traumatic Stress Network (NCTSN). Through her leadership, trauma-informed care is not just a buzzword—it's an operating principle.

As the field continues to evolve, innovations are emerging across diverse platforms:

- Telehealth and hybrid care models have made therapy more accessible, especially for those in remote or underserved areas.
- Somatic and neurobiological interventions, such as EMDR, polyvagal theory-informed practice, and expressive arts therapies, are redefining what healing looks and feels like.
- Community-based participatory models are being applied not only in public health, but also in community organizing, peer-led services, and reentry programs.
- Technology-assisted interventions, including mental health apps, digital journaling tools, and AI-supported assessments, are on the rise—raising both opportunities and ethical questions.
- Narrative, spiritual, and culturally-rooted modalities are being reclaimed and re-integrated into mainstream care, especially by BIPOC, LGBTQ+, and immigrant clinicians.

But perhaps the greatest innovation lies not in any one technique, but in the rediscovery of community. Whether it is the kinship fostered at the SWEET Institute, or the grassroots collectives advocating for change on the ground, clinicians are remembering that healing is never solitary. It is relational. And in that space between one heart and another, the future is being written—not just imagined, but lived.

Chapter 56: Challenges Facing the Field

Despite the promising innovations reshaping social work, the field faces persistent and profound challenges. These are not new—but they are increasingly urgent. From systemic underfunding to vicarious trauma, and from professional devaluation to structural inequities, social workers must often navigate environments that drain the very empathy they are called to give. These challenges, however, are not signs of failure. They are the growing pains of a profession in transformation—painful, yes, but also full of potential.

Jenna reflects on this tension with characteristic clarity. Though her work is rooted in trauma-informed systems, she is deeply aware that systemic implementation often lags behind policy rhetoric. "It's one thing to train people in trauma-informed care," she notes. "It's another to create a culture that consistently models safety, trustworthiness, and empowerment." Her observation echoes what organizational theorists call implementation fatigue—the gap between what is promised in mission statements and what is resourced in practice (Fixsen et al., 2005).

Olivia highlights the enduring inequities that remain within the field—both for the people social workers serve and for the social workers themselves. "Access to therapy should not be a privilege," she asserts. But she also points to burnout and compassion fatigue as critical issues among clinicians, particularly BIPOC and frontline workers. Her insights align with recent research on empathic distress fatigue, which shows that professionals who work with high-need populations in low-resource settings often internalize systemic suffering without adequate institutional support (Rothschild, 2006; Figley, 1995).

Lorie, whose decades in the field have made her both a seasoned therapist and an educator, emphasizes the emotional toll of witnessing repeated systemic failures. "You see families fall through the cracks—again and again. You see brilliant clinicians leave the field because the systems don't support them." Her perspective underscores the need for collective trauma literacy—not only to serve clients, but to care for ourselves and our colleagues.

Across these voices, common themes emerge—challenges that are structural, cultural, and existential:

- Workforce instability: Low pay, high caseloads, and poor supervision contribute to high turnover, especially in community-based settings.
- Systemic racism and exclusion: BIPOC practitioners continue to report microaggressions, inequitable promotion, and tokenism, even within so-called progressive organizations.
- Fragmentation of services: Clients are often bounced between providers, with no continuity of care—particularly at the intersection of mental health, housing, criminal justice, and education systems.
- Bureaucratic overload: Excessive documentation and compliance requirements hinder creative, relational, and therapeutic work.
- Isolation and moral injury: Many clinicians work alone, in silos, facing ethical dilemmas without support or space for reflection.

And yet, within these challenges lies the seed of transformation.

The SWEET Institute, for example, offers more than just tools. It offers community infrastructure. By creating space for reflection, connection, and accountability, it models an alternative to the burnout cycle. It reminds clinicians that we don't have to hold the world alone—and that perhaps the most radical thing we can do in a broken system is to heal in relationship, together.

These challenges are not just obstacles. They are calls to action. And those who answer them—clinicians like Jenna, Olivia, and Lorie—are helping the field move forward not despite adversity, but through it.

Chapter 57: The Role of Technology and Systems Change

The social work field, long associated with face-to-face, heart-to-heart engagement, is undergoing a seismic shift. Technology, once seen as peripheral or even antithetical to the relational nature of our work, is now at the center of conversations about access, equity, and systems change. And while this evolution brings enormous promise, it also demands deep discernment.

For many clinicians, the pandemic was a portal—a moment when the impossible (fully virtual therapy, telehealth for underserved populations, online education) became not only possible, but necessary. As Olivia reflects, "Learning to navigate virtual therapy wasn't just a logistical pivot—it was a paradigm shift. Suddenly, we had to ask ourselves: What does presence mean in a digital space?" Her experience mirrors what scholars of digital mental health have termed relational presence at a distance—the ability to cultivate therapeutic connection even without physical proximity (Gibson et al., 2020).

Jenna, whose leadership has spanned in-person programming and virtual innovation, sees this moment as a rare opportunity for systemic integration. "We can't go back to the old silos. Technology, when used ethically and equitably, can help us create wraparound systems that actually talk to each other." She envisions platforms that allow for seamless communication between schools, mental health providers, housing coordinators, and justice systems—what health systems scholars call interoperability for coordinated care (Valentijn et al., 2013).

At the same time, these opportunities come with real risks. Lorie warns against allowing efficiency to eclipse empathy. "Just because we can use an app or automate something doesn't mean we should. We need to keep the human at the center." Her concern echoes critiques of algorithmic decision-making in child welfare and criminal justice—areas where predictive analytics have sometimes reinforced, rather than reduced, systemic bias (Eubanks, 2018).

The clinicians aligned with the SWEET Institute offer a grounded, visionary approach to integrating technology and systems change. Rather than rushing toward the latest tech trend, they emphasize the importance of values-driven implementation:

- Technology as a tool for equity: Increasing access for rural, disabled, and low-income clients.
- Data-informed but not data-dominated: Using metrics to inform care, not dictate it.
- Platforms for practitioner support: Communities like SWEET offer virtual spaces for connection, supervision, and reflection—mitigating the isolation of digital practice.
- Client voice in digital design: Including those we serve in the development of apps, platforms, and systems.

Ultimately, this chapter in social work's evolution is not about replacing the human touch with machines. It's about enhancing our reach, our coordination, and our impact—while holding fast to the core values that make social work what it is.

Technology won't solve systemic problems by itself. But when coupled with collective wisdom, ethical clarity, and practitioner-led innovation, it becomes a powerful ally in reimagining the systems we so urgently need to change.

Chapter 58: Trauma-Informed and Human-Centered Futures

The future of social work is not merely about innovation—it is about intention. As the field continues to evolve, clinicians across the SWEET Institute community envision a future that places human dignity, safety, and resilience at its very core. At the heart of that vision is a deep commitment to trauma-informed and human-centered approaches.

Jenna, whose career has long centered on trauma-informed practice, believes that this framework must be more than a buzzword. "It's not just about understanding trauma," she says, "it's about rethinking our systems so they stop causing it." Her work pushes institutions to move beyond trauma awareness into trauma responsiveness—a shift that demands not just knowledge but systemic accountability.

Lorie echoes this call. Drawing from her experience integrating cognitive-behavioral therapy with strength-based, person-centered methods, she sees trauma-informed care as a philosophy of engagement. "People are not their diagnoses," she reminds us. "We must treat every client as someone who already holds the seeds of their own healing." This aligns with a growing body of research emphasizing empowerment, choice, and relational safety as core elements of effective trauma treatment (Fallot & Harris, 2009; SAMHSA, 2014).

At the SWEET Institute, these principles are not confined to clinical sessions—they permeate how clinicians learn, grow, and support one another. The very structure of the Institute—with its emphasis on reflection, community, and mutual regard—is itself trauma-informed. It offers a model of continuing education that mirrors the values we hope to bring into therapeutic spaces: empathy, safety, empowerment, and respect for lived experience.

Olivia, who practices somatic and mindfulness-based therapies, sees a shift happening. "More clinicians are finally recognizing that trauma lives in the body—not just in thoughts or behaviors," she notes. "We need approaches that honor the whole person." The SWEET Institute's integration of evidence-based models with holistic perspectives reflects this shift. Modalities like EMDR, DBT, ACT, and body-based work are not viewed as separate silos but as interconnected tools for healing.

This chapter in the evolution of social work calls for a new kind of clinician: one who can navigate systems, hold space for pain, question oppressive structures, and embody the very change they hope to inspire. It is a tall order—and yet, as these clinicians demonstrate, it is also deeply possible.

As the field moves forward, trauma-informed and human-centered care will not be optional add-ons. They will be the foundation upon which all sustainable, ethical, and transformative practice is built.

Because the future of social work is not just about what we do. It's about how we do it—and who we become while doing it.

Chapter 59: Advocacy, Policy, and Collective Power

Social work has always been rooted in advocacy—but never has the need for collective power been more urgent. As systemic inequities persist across healthcare, housing, education, and the justice system, today's clinicians are reclaiming their roles as policy shapers, not just service providers. The future of social work, as envisioned by members of the SWEET Institute, lies in leveraging clinical insight to drive structural change.

For Jenna, this connection is deeply personal. Her leadership in trauma-informed care has expanded into broader systems change, influencing policies and programming across agencies. "We have to stop thinking of social work as limited to therapy rooms or case files," she explains. "The systems we work in—schools, courts, hospitals—must be transformed too. And we are the ones who can help lead that transformation." Her work demonstrates how clinical insight, when paired with advocacy, can redesign environments to be more just and responsive.

Denise echoes this conviction. With decades of experience navigating public mental health systems, she has long recognized that individual healing cannot be separated from systemic reform. "We're trained to be aware of power," she says. "But awareness isn't enough. We need to act. Whether it's lobbying for trauma-informed legislation, fighting for housing equity, or challenging policies that criminalize mental illness—we must be at the table."

At the SWEET Institute, this ethos is not an afterthought—it is embedded in the very structure of learning. Through courses, discussions, and community accountability, clinicians are invited to explore not only their therapeutic skills but their civic responsibility. The Institute's emphasis on critical thinking and conscious-based intervention equips members to challenge status quos while fostering collective imagination.

Doug, whose background in both law and social work offers a dual lens, views the SWEET Institute as a rare space where policy and practice converge. "Most educational platforms don't bridge the gap," he says. "But SWEET does. It gives us the tools to understand systems—and the courage to change them."

Guillermina, grounded in both school-based work and early intervention, believes that policy advocacy must begin with those most often overlooked. "It's not just about writing letters or attending rallies," she reflects. "It's about amplifying the voices of children, parents, immigrants, and elders who live with the daily impact of broken systems."

In this future, advocacy is no longer siloed—it is integrated into everyday practice. It becomes a form of ethical alignment, ensuring that our interventions don't just soothe symptoms but challenge root causes.

And collective power becomes the engine. Not the power of one voice alone, but of many—linked by shared purpose, professional values, and a vision for justice.

Because in the end, the future of social work will not be written by policymakers alone.

It will be written by clinicians who refuse to separate healing from justice.

Concluding Reflection – Section VII: The Vision Forward

As this section draws to a close, one truth rises above all others: social work is not standing still—it is evolving, expanding, and rising to meet the complexity of our time. From healing trauma to transforming systems, from cultivating empathy to demanding equity, the vision shared by these clinicians is bold, human-centered, and rooted in deep integrity.

They remind us that the future of social work is not just about more tools—it's about more courage. Not just better systems—but reimagined ones. It is about clinicians who recognize that their role is both intimate and expansive—bridging the personal and the political, the therapeutic and the structural, the now and the not-yet.

The SWEET Institute has been more than a witness to this evolution—it has been an incubator of it. In classrooms and communities, it has nurtured a generation of professionals who are not only clinically skilled, but socially conscious and unapologetically visionary.

And so, the path forward is not one of uncertainty, but of promise.

Social work, at its best, has always held the capacity to heal what is broken—within individuals, families, and society. This section affirms that this calling is not only alive—it is being redefined, expanded, and led with purpose.

Let us follow their lead.

Let us build what is next.

Concluding Reflection – The Journey Home

From the first moment a clinician feels the quiet tug toward service—to the long, complex, and often sacred work of walking beside others through pain, possibility, and transformation—social work has never been just a profession. It is a calling. A way of being. A deeply human response to suffering, injustice, and the unyielding hope that healing is always possible.

This book has taken us through that journey—from the first spark of purpose, to the hard-won lessons of experience, the craft of clinical practice, the anchoring of community, and the integration of personal meaning. Each story, each voice, has illuminated a path that is rarely linear but always rich with truth.

In these pages, we have seen resilience redefined. We have watched values come alive. We have witnessed what it means to stay—through doubt, through hardship, through changing systems and shifting roles. And we have seen what is possible when clinicians are not only trained but held, not only challenged but inspired, not only informed but transformed.

The SWEET Institute has offered more than a platform for learning—it has offered a place of remembering. A remembering of why we do this work. A remembering of the power of presence, the necessity of justice, and the infinite potential of the human spirit.

To every clinician who has shared their story: thank you. You have not only honored your own journey—you have lit the way for others.

To the reader: may this book remind you that you are not alone. That your work matters. That your being matters. That in a world fractured by fear and disconnection, the act of showing up—with curiosity, courage, and care—is itself a revolution.

Let this not be the end, but a beginning.

Let us walk forward—together—with clarity, compassion, and the unshakable belief that healing is not only our work. It is our legacy.

Recommended Reading

Further Exploration of Healing, Hope, and the Power of Social Work

These books, articles, and texts reflect the spirit of The Courage to Care—spanning clinical wisdom, systemic insight, social justice, and personal growth. They have inspired many of the contributors and align with the vision of the SWEET Institute.

On the Power and Practice of Social Work

- The Social Work Values and Ethics Handbook – Frederic Reamer
- Social Work Matters: The Power of Linking Policy and Practice – Elizabeth F. Hoffler & Elizabeth J. Clark
- The Spirit Catches You and You Fall Down – Anne Fadiman
- Trauma Stewardship: An Everyday Guide to Caring for Self While Caring for Others – Laura van Dernoot Lipsky & Connie Burk

On Mental Health, Healing, and Therapy

- Man's Search for Meaning – Viktor E. Frankl
- The Body Keeps the Score – Bessel van der Kolk, M.D.
- My Grandmother's Hands – Resmaa Menakem
- The Gift of Therapy – Irvin D. Yalom, M.D.
- What Happened to You? – Dr. Bruce Perry & Oprah Winfrey

On Equity, Justice, and Cultural Humility

- The New Jim Crow – Michelle Alexander
- So You Want to Talk About Race – Ijeoma Oluo
- Decolonizing Trauma Work – Renee Linklater

- Sister Outsider – Audre Lorde
- Pedagogy of the Oppressed – Paulo Freire

On Leadership, Systems, and Transformation

- Leaders Eat Last – Simon Sinek
- Systems Thinking for Social Change – David Peter Stroh
- The Art of Possibility – Rosamund Stone Zander & Benjamin Zander

This book was brought to life by members of the SWEET Institute and edited by Karen Dubin, Ph.D., LCSW and Mardoche Sidor, MD, who, together with the 50 clinicians featured in this book, are committed to transforming mental health from the inside out.

Below is a selection of recommended resources, trainings, and publications authored by SWEET Institute leaders and collaborators.

Books to look out for by the Authors

- Before Anything Else, Validate (forthcoming)
- A practical guide to transforming relationships and healing through radical validation.
- By Mardoche Sidor, MD and Karen Dubin, Ph.D., LCSW
- The Still Point (forthcoming)
- A poetic journey into the power of presence in clinical care and human transformation.
- How Life Works (forthcoming)
- 20 timeless lessons for living with meaning, healing the past, and stepping into authentic power.
- By Mardoche Sidor, MD and Karen Dubin, Ph.D., LCSW
- The Clinician's Mirror (forthcoming)

- Exploring projection, shadow work, and the art of becoming a healing presence.

Signature Trainings from SWEET Institute

- The SWEET Psychotherapy Certificate Program
- A year-long immersion into healing through presence, behavior change, cognitive tools, and emotional awareness.
- Motivational Interviewing Certificate Course
- Person-centered communication strategies for helping people change—offered with trauma-informed and neurodevelopmental integrations.
- SWEET Healing Circles
- Experiential spaces for clinicians and community members to gather, reflect, and transform—offered quarterly.
- SWEET Supervision and Clinical Coaching Certification
- Learn the art of facilitating growth, accountability, and insight in others.

Articles and Reflections by the Authors

You can read selected essays, articles, and thought pieces from the SWEET Institute and its clinicians at: https://sweetinstitute.com/blog/

Some reader favorites include:

- "Reparenting the Inner Child"
- "The Truth and Challenges of Trauma-Informed Care"
- "Healing Inner Child Wounds"
- "Purpose: Finding What You're Best At"

Stay Connected

- Join SWEET as a Member:
    - Access live weekly trainings, earn CEUs, join supervision circles, and become part of a national movement at www.sweetinstitute.com/membership
- Follow SWEET on Social Media:
    - [LinkedIn | Facebook | YouTube]
- Check Out our Weekly Reflection Series:
    - https://sweetinstitute.com/blog/